GEMATRIA
The Numbers of Infinity

Marke Pawson

Green Magic

This edition is published by

Green Magic
Long Barn
Sutton Mallet
TA7 9AR
England

Typeset by Academic + Technical, Bristol
Printed and bound by Antony Rowe Ltd, Chippenham

Cover design: Chris Render
Technical assistance: M. Gotto
Cover production: Tania Lambert

www.life-tree.co.uk (Marke Pawson)

ISBN 0 9547 2300 7

GREEN MAGIC

CONTENTS

INTRODUCTION

The Bible and, in particular, the Old Testament, is quite simply the most important book in the English language. This is, of course, a complete contradiction of the received view in present-day scientific circles, where the Bible is seen as having no relevance at all to conventional science. However, modern physicists, for example, will admit that there are certain fundamental questions that they cannot answer – one of these concerns the nature of gravity. The effects of gravity are universal in the physical world, but the means by which it is expressed are unknown: unlike, for example, the photon in light. No one has ever demonstrated the existence of a graviton, but physicists know that if a gravity particle does not exist, the whole edifice of modern physics collapses. Well, anyone reading this book will discover that whoever wrote the Bible knew all about gravity and how to manipulate it for both constructive and destructive purposes.

Another question facing science today is the possibility of discovering an all-inclusive theory, something that explains all perceived phenomena. Einstein looked for it without success and others are still looking. This book demonstrates that, with an understanding of the science of gematria, a final, all-inclusive theory is revealed in the Hebrew text of the Old Testament.

Beautifully poetic as the text of the King James English version is, the immense wisdom that the authors wished to impart lies in the Hebrew text. So why is this text so important? The answer lies in the fact that the letters of the Hebrew AlephBayt also serve as numbers, so that any word or phrase written in Hebrew has a numerical value. This forms the basis of the science of Gematria.

Bezalel, who designed the tabernacle to contain the Ark of the Covenant, could, according to Hebrew myth, "use letters as instruments of power". Gematria reveals a coherent pattern of creative energy concealed in the text. This in turn leads us to an understanding of the creative process by which our whole Universe is formed.

About three thousand years ago, when the authors of the Torah decided to put their wisdom into writing, they looked at the instrument available for their purpose, the Hebrew AlephBayt of twenty-two letters. For some reason it wasn't, as they saw it, quite right for their needs and they decided to add five letters, to make twenty-seven. These extra letters are called 'finals' and are different versions of five of the twenty-two letters already existing, so that, when one of these five letters occurs at the end of a word, the final version is used. Why did they do this? It doesn't make the text any easier to understand and why only five? Why not design a final version for all twenty-two?

The answer is revealed in Figure 1. Stan Tenen of the Meru Foundation[1] realised that a $2 \times 2 \times 2$ cube, composed of eight cubic modules, has twenty-seven points of intersection, one for each of letter of the

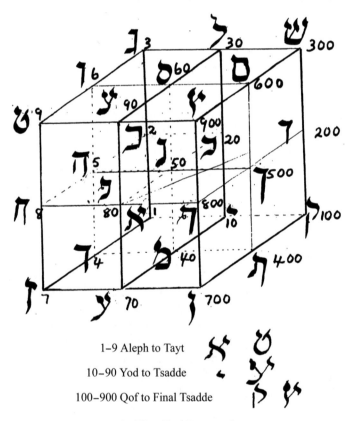

1–9 Aleph to Tayt

10–90 Yod to Tsadde

100–900 Qof to Final Tsadde

Figure 1. The AlephBaytic cube.

vi

AlephBayt. He developed a Base 3 code from this, derived from the three axes of the cube. Figure 1 shows the cube with the letters in their positions and their gematria.

The gematria of the whole AlephBayt is divided into three groups: letters with numbers from 1 to 9, those from 10 to 90 and those from 100 to 900. Figure 1 shows that each of these groups lies in a vertical plane within the cube. This supports the theory that the AlephBayt was designed to fit the $2 \times 2 \times 2$ cube and explains why the authors needed the five extra letters. The whole science of gematria is built around this cube of letters and every word and phrase can be expressed in this three-dimensional structure.

The Greek alphabet, which may have evolved from the same source as the AlephBayt, was likewise developed "in order to have sufficient symbols to accommodate the denary system of numeration".[2] Like the Hebrew version, there are three groups of nine letters, representing the numbers 1 to 9, 10 to 90 and 100 to 900. However, the evolution of the Greek system before the Christian Era (BCE) differed fundamentally from that of the Hebrew. Whereas the Hebrew system was deliberately *increased* from 22 to 27 symbols, by the time the New Testament came to be written three letters had been lost from the Greek alphabet, so that each of the three groups of letters contained only eight. It is this defective alphabet which forms the basis of Bligh Bond and Simcox Lea's investigation of the gematria of the New Testament.

When Bond and Lea wrote their book *Gematria*, about 80 years ago, the matter of the missing letters could be regarded as a mere technicality, but Stan Tenen's discovery of the AlephBaytic cube of twenty-seven letters has completely changed the position. It makes it essential, as anyone reading this book will discover, that there should be twenty-seven letters.

The translation of the Greek in the first chapter of Revelation, "I am Alpha and Omega, the first and the last, the beginning and the end",[3] where the letter Omega in gematria has the value 800, can be written in Hebrew and translated into English as "I am Aleph and Final Tsadde, the first and the last", Final Tsadde having the gematria 900. A glance at Figure 1 shows that Final Tsadde lies at the diagonally opposite corner to Aleph, completing the cube, while Omega, with a value of 800, lies in the middle of one edge, so that the cube is incomplete on the basis of the Greek.

In our society the fate of the Bible is either to be ignored or misused – misused through ignorance, for example with the portrayal of a capricious, sometime vengeful tribal deity; sometimes deliberately as a justification for the persecution of those who do not share one particular morality; or as the basis for a code of practice for society.

This was the situation when Bond and Lea published *Gematria* in the early part of the last century. In the early days of Christianity, Christian Gnostics combined the ancient wisdom underlying all the sacred books, such as the Torah, the Rg Veda and the Popul Vuh, with the teachings of the New Testament, employing the science of Gematria in the Greek text. All this was soon suppressed, or concealed by orthodox Christians, who, in their ignorance, regarded it as heresy.

So it was that Bond and Lea revealed a totally different view of Christianity that had been lost for eighteen hundred years, one in which "the principles of Number, Sound (music) and Form (geometry) are connected with each letter".[4] For example, in the case of geometry, "in the numbers titles and epithets of Our Lord" and His Mother, these refer to cubes of one, two and four. What Bond and Lea were apparently not aware of was that the second of these, the $2 \times 2 \times 2$ cube, contains 27 points, one for each letter of the Hebrew AlephBayt. Stan Tenen, of the Meru Foundation, was the first to publish this discovery in 1981. This, as we shall see, places Bond and Lea's work in a completely new light, since significant words and phrases in the Hebrew text of the Torah etc. can now be placed in the cube so that they give rise to three-dimensional structures. Figure 2 shows an example of the application of this method, using the Hebrew for the sacred name of God, Aleph Hay Yod Hay.[5] This drawing emphasises one of the eight cubic modules that make up the whole AlephBaytic cube. By linking up the first pair of letters in the Hebrew word, Aleph Hay, we get a diagonal across a face of the module, while linking the second pair, Yod Hay, we get the internal diagonal of the module. Then if the length of each side of the module is equal to 1, the diagonal of the face equals 1×2 and the internal diagonal equals $1 \times \sqrt{3}$. Here we have an illustration of the connection between the letters in key words in the text and the operation of principles of number, the roots in relation to 1, Sound (the spoken word) and Geometry (the cube).[6]

We have here a system in which the letters represent energies, which are combined in words and phrases, and these in turn are built into three-dimensional patterns expressed in forms with crystalline, musical and geometric proportions. Of course this is all completely foreign to our understanding of language today, which is regarded as a means of conveying facts and theories and expressing ideas and feelings. However, Hebrew mythology and the Hebrew text of the Torah support the concept of letters as energetic tools in the creative process. "And Moses said unto the children of Israel, See, the Lord hath called by name, Bezalel of the tribe of Judah; and he hath filled him with the spirit of God, in wisdom, and understanding and in knowledge and to

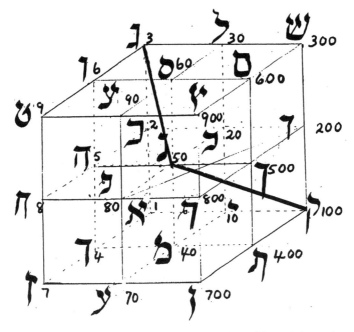

Figure 2. Bezalel: the hologram for the cube. One hundred, fifty and three, the gematria of Bezalel in Hebrew, points to the centre and two corners of the cube.

devise cunning works".[7] The next few chapters of Exodus describe how Bezalel and his partner Aholiab designed, built and furnished the tabernacle, the centre of the people's life during the journey to Canaan.

In the Hebrew text Bezalel is written as Bayt Tsadde Lammed Aleph Lammed, whose numbers in gematria are 2, 90, 30, 1 and 30, giving a total of 153, or "One hundred, fifty and three",[8] referring respectively to the letters Qof, Nun and Ghimel in the AlephBaytic cube. Reference to the cube, shown in Figure 2, reveals that the letter Nun is at the centre of the cube and that Ghimel and Qof are at two of its corners. Together they make a hologram, a minimum resolution figure for the construction of the cube. Thus Bezalel embodies in his name the information necessary to construct the tabernacle.

Looking at the position of these three letters, Nun, Ghimel and Qof, as they appear in Figure 7, we can see that they form the corners of an isosceles triangle whose base, Ghimel Qof, forms a diagonal on one of the faces of the cube, with the apex of the triangle at the centre of the cube, Nun. In the base Ghimel Qof is equal to $1 \times \sqrt{2}$, then the length of the other two sides is equal to $1 \times \sqrt{3}/2$, or $1 \times 1.73/2$, since each side makes half an internal diagonal within the cube and the latter is equal to the length of one side $\times \sqrt{3}$. $1.73/2 = 0.865$ and in gematria decimal points are disregarded, so we can call the number 865. By the rule of Colel in gematria, in which a margin of ± 1 is allowed, we can call this 864, which is the gematria of the Greek 'Kyrios demei', "The Lord builds (His tabernacle)".[9] We can see that the gematria tie Bezalel in with the building of the tabernacle and the proportions of the cube of letters in two different ways.

The name Bezalel (Bezal. El) means Lord or Master of the Curve, referring to the calligraphic curve, or the art of calligraphy. But extra-Biblical Hebrew myth states that Bezalel knew how to use the symbols of the AlephBayt as creative instruments and these are the "cunning works" referred to in Exodus 30:32. This justifies the claim made by Jews that their system of letters is different from others; underlying its practical purpose it enables those with understanding to put the letters together in words and phrases, which enable creative energies to be organised so as to create physical form.

Those who set out to write down the Torah knew this and designed a system of symbols which could then be put together in the text in order to convey to those with understanding the secret of the whole creative process. This underlying truth is a fundamental distinction between sacred texts, such as the Hebrew and Greek texts of the Bible and other written works. Bligh Bond and Lea understood this and they demonstrate its expression in the science of gematria in arithmetic, geometric and musical terms. However, lacking a knowledge of the AlephBaytic cube, they were unable to show the link between the higher/non-physical energies and the three-dimensional, which the Hebrew and Greek texts reveal in conjunction with the cube of letters.

Bond and Lea give examples of Greek words whose gematria relate to cubic proportions:[10]

1. Kephas, a name given to Peter by Jesus, whose gematria is $729 = 9 \times 9 \times 9$. "Kephas" is the perfect ashlar stone, or cubic stone. Peter became the foundation of the Christian Church.[11]
2. To thysiasterion, the altar $= 12 \times 12 \times 12$, the early Christian altars being cubic. The altar in Hebrew is Mem Zayn Bayt, whose gematria is $49 = 7 \times 7$, suggesting one, the upper surface of the cube. A Hebrew word referring to the space containing the altar, the Debir, or Most Holy Place, is 216 in gematria, or $6 \times 6 \times 6$.

Bond and Lea also refer to the Agiasma, the Greek sanctuary, whose gematria is 256, or $4 \times 4 \times 4 \times 4$, "embodying, in addition to the Cube, a transcendental fourth measure" and this fourth measure suggests the higher energies represented by the roots of the number one in the proportions of the AlephBaytic cube.

"And within the oracle was a space of twenty cubits in length, and twenty cubits in breadth, and twenty cubits in the height thereof".[12] Here, in the Hebrew version of this passage, the word translated as 'oracle' in the 1611 and 1885 versions, is 'Debir', the Most Holy Place in the Hebrew temple, so that the Greek Agiasma, the sanctuary, or place devoted to the gods in the Greek temple, corresponds to the Hebrew Most Holy Place. The higher dimension suggested by Agiasma's gematria of $4 \times 4 \times 4 \times 4$ clearly refers to the presence of non-physical energies, referred to as 'God' or 'the gods'.

The way in which the gematria of all these terms refers to the cube and their association with the inner part of the temple, in both the Hebrew and Greek religious practice, underlines the significance of the AlephBaytic cube in the process of translating higher energies into three-dimensional form. Stan Tenen's discovery of the cube of Hebrew letters and its employment in conjunction with the Hebrew text and the gematria of the latter, opens up immense possibilities for an understanding of the esoteric meaning of the text.

"Both Greek and Hebrew modes of numeration are based on a denary system: that is to say, one which divides into units, tens, hundreds etc., but it must be born in mind that the use of the 0, or zero was not then known ...".[13] It is true that, in a strictly arithmetic sense, 0 was unknown but, in a wider context, it plays a very significant part. In the Cabalistic Tree of Life, the Prima Sephira, from which the rest of the tree may be said to grow, consists essentially of a 0 containing a 1. This represents the resting state, in a botanic sense the seed, cosmically the Night of Brahma, according to the Vedic system. The 1 within the 0 is the Omphalos, or Cosmic Phallus, the creative instrument, at this stage contained within the Cosmic Egg.

The active phase, the Day of Brahma, is initiated by the emergence of the phallus, so that we have

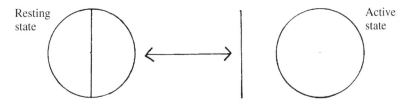

This then gives rise to the 10 Sephiroth of the Tree of Life, the foundation of the denary system.

Bond and Lea[14] go on to look at numbers "expressive of the circum-ference of circles in relation to their diameters". An example of this is the Greek word epithymia, meaning desire, whose gematria is 555 ($= 37 \times 15$). A circle whose diameter is 555 has a circumference of 1746 ($\pi \times 555$), which is the gematria of the Greek 'kokkos sinapeos', a mustard seed, "the least of all the seeds, from which sprang a great tree".[15] This "great tree" is clearly the Tree of Life, and in the Greek text 'tree' is dendron, whose gematria is 283, while that of Theos (God) is 284. Here 'God' is expressed by the Prima Sephira, the source of all things. A circle whose diameter is 284 has a circumference of 891, the gematria of the Greek 'Ouranos' (heaven), which brings us back to Revelation 21 and the manifestation of the New Jerusalem.

In the Prima Sephira the resting state shown above, the 1 contained within the 0 in this example is equal to 555, the gematria of the Greek 'epithymia', meaning desire. It may be said to be desire that motivates the Creative Source to project the Cosmic Phallus, the 1, setting in motion an active, creative, phase.

Here we have "typical illustrations of the Geometric Method" and its arithmetical basis in the Prima Sephira. Bond and Lea refer to Gnostic works, such as the Books of Ieou and the Pistis Sophia, as being full of examples of this underlying geometry, occurring as "part of a more coherent teaching".[16] As we shall see, the Hebrew text of the Torah and the rest of the Old Testament also reveal this coherent teaching and their coherence extends to musical proportion and crystal structure, all revealed by the gematria of the key words and phrases of the Hebrew text.

1

CUTTING THE THEOLOGICAL BONDS

There is nothing foreign to the use of gematria "in the idea that our Lord did actually use the geometry, such as any builder might have knowledge of, for the building up of the wisdom of His Church".[1] Anyone reading this book will quickly become aware that it has implications that extend beyond the limits set by the Christian church, or those of any other belief system. Their exposition suggests that Bond and Lea were aware of this, even if they were unwilling to make a catagorical statement to this effect.

"The phenomenon of Life – appearing first as a microscopic germ, yet holding within itself the potentiality of growth and infinite reproduction, engender this thought – from what unseen source does it arrive?"[2] On page 8 of *Gematria*, Bond and Lea give an alternative form for gematria as gametria, suggesting the Greek gametia, a wife, and gametes, a husband, whose unipolar gametes, the sperm and the egg, combine to form the new bipolar offspring. This process of conception is, in the Greek, katabolē, literally 'throwing down', the descent of the soul from some higher realm. As we shall see, this word katabolē is a key term in the geometry associated with the Cabala.[3]

"Now did the early Christians hold ideas of higher dimensions of space?"[4] Such ideas are clearly suggested in the Old Testament, for example, in the account of Jacob's dream, "And [Jacob] dreamed, and behold a ladder set up on the earth, and the top of it reached to heaven: and behold the angels of god ascending and descending on it".[5] Here we have a hierarchy of energy levels (frequency ranges) or dimensions, extending between the highest, indicated by heaven, with the rungs of the ladder indicating the intermediate frequency levels, or dimensions and the bottom of the ladder resting on the earth, the lowest frequency. The word 'angels' in the English text is a translation of the Greek 'āggelos', meaning 'messenger'; they indicate the flow of energy. The word 'āggelos' has the gematria 312, as does the word 'dēlos', meaning manifestation and it is the descent of the energy to the lowest level, our physical universe, which leads to the manifestation of material form.

Here Bond and Lea refer to "the spiritual possessions with which the Christian religion endowed its converts"[6] among which was a Knowledge, described by the Greek term 'Gnosis'. Looking at their work 80 or so years later, it does not seem helpful to look at such a body of spiritual understanding from a strictly Christian standpoint. If we agree to discard this limitation, then the gematria of the Hebrew text of the Old Testament reveals a gnosis in the form of a coherent body of spiritual understanding running through the whole text. An example of this lies in the third chapter of Genesis, but, as Carlo Suares points out, the English text is riddled with corruptions. For example, Suares states "Tov (translated as 'good') really means limited in its material proliferation and the process Raa (translated as 'evil') is really a loosening of our bonds, an awakening or quickening of the life force. One can understand that the action of Raa, far from being in any sense evil, is designed to save our life".[7] The English translation presents the serpent as the embodiment of evil. In reality it symbolises creative energy and the Hebrew word, Hanahhash, has the gematria 363 and the Greek phrase 'victory of truth' has the gematria 360. Furthermore, in verse 13, the phrase translated as "the serpent beguiled", in the Hebrew has the gematria 739 and 740 is the gematria of the Greek 'ktisis', meaning 'creation', confirming the creative nature of the serpent. Then the word translated as 'woman' is Esha in the Hebrew has the gematria 312, the same as that of the Greek 'dēlos', 'manifestation', indicating that the creation is manifested through the woman. All this not only reveals the corrupt nature of the English text, but also demonstrates the way in which the gematria preserve and reveal the true meaning. We can now see how Esha, the feminine, embodies the serpentine creative energy and manifests it as physical form.

In the account of Jacob's dream we saw that the Angels (in Greek 'āggelos'), symbolised the same creative energy flowing up and down the ladder and, like Esha, 'āggelos' also has the gematria 312. All this illustrates one important function of gematria: ever since translations of the Hebrew text began to be made, into Greek, Latin and then into modern languages, corruptions of the Hebrew text have crept in and accumulated over the centuries, some due to mistakes made by the scribes, others as a result of a deliberate intention to alter the meaning. The above example is a case of the latter. The Christian Church has promoted the idea of humanity as 'born in sin' and that it is womankind that is responsible for that sinful state. By going back to the Hebrew text

2

and working with the gematria of key words and phrases, such as Hanah-hash Hashayiny ("The serpent beguiled me" in the King James version), we can see how the gematria reveal the creative energy, symbolised by the 'serpent', works through the woman as an instrument of the creative process. As Bond and Lea state, "Number and Geometrical form are aeonically [agelessly] true and constant in their relations, and a system of representation of natural truth having for its vehicle a carefully co-ordinated series of number symbols",[8] such as that of the science of gematria, will act to preserve the true meaning of the original text. A philosophy and system of ideas, such as expressed in the Hebrew text of the Old Testament, "is not capable of clear expression in terms of human language...but a mathematical expression may be found for this". When this mathematical expression can be shown to run coherently through the whole text, its validity is hard to challenge.

In verse 20 of the third chapter of Genesis Eve appears, although readers of the English text usually assume that the 'woman' in the earlier part of the chapter and Eve are synonymous. The Hebrew text makes it clear that they are not – Esha, the woman, as we have seen, being a cosmic entity, while Eve suggests a human individual. In Hebrew her name is written as Hhayt Vav Hay, whose gematria is 19. Bond and Lea describe a series of cubes that they call Metacubes.[9] The second of these, a $2 \times 2 \times 2$ cube, 'the Cube of the Mother', has 27 points, of which 19 are visible. "456 then is the number of visible points, each counted as 24" and 456 is the gematria of 'mētēr' [mother]. As we have seen, this cube, with its total of 27 points, is the AlephBaytic cube, with one point for each letter of the alphabet, by means of which the words and phrases of the Hebrew text are translated into three-dimensional form.

In Appendix D of their book, Bond and Lea show the Metacube as three concentric rings, with a central point and successively 6, 12 and 18 points. They give each point a value of 24 and then look at the gematria of a number of significant words and phrases whose gematria are multi-ples of 24.[10] Clearly this number is significant, but they do not explain why. The explanation of the importance of 24 lies in the Book of Revelation where we have "And round about the throne...four and twenty elders...and the four and twenty elders fell down and worshipped...".[11] In Hebrew 'Elder' is Zayn Qof Nun Yod, whose gematria is 167 and $168 = 7 \times 24$, a reference to Bond and Lea's three concentric rings, specifically the central point and the six points of the inner ring. We have here an energy system based on a frequency repre-sented by the number 24. The sources of energy are laid out in concentric circles. The phrase "bowed down and worshipped" indicates energy flowing from the 'Elders' into the throne at the centre, the central point in Bond and Lea's diagram. They go on to show a large number of Greek words whose gematria are multiples of 24. In his book *God's Secret Formula*, Peter Plichta uses a purely arithmetical method to work towards a similar solution. He uses concentric rings of numbers, 24 in each, 1 to 24, 25 to 48 and so on, demonstrating that the distribution of prime numbers is not a random one, but shows a pattern.[12] It is not by chance that the number 37, which is the arithmetic base for most of Bond and Lea's work, is a prime number. All except one of their "Numbers of Perfection" (page 42) 7, 13, 19, 25, 31, 37 and 43, are prime numbers (see Figure 17).

The authors acknowledge that "to work from translations is never satisfactory"[13] and, by implication, they recognise the superiority of the Hebrew text. They discuss the alternative spellings of the name John, one of which, Ioannes, only differs in its initial I from the name of the Sumerian half man, half fish, who taught mankind the arts of civilisation. They confirm the link by pointing out that "the Chaldean Noah, Xisuthrus, written in Greek, has the gematria 1119", the same as that of Ioannes. According to Sumerian myth, Xisuthrus, or Oannes, was one of a number of amphibious beings who descended to earth and had to return to the water each night. This hints at the origin of the practice of baptism and explains the association of Ioannes (John the Baptist) with this ritual.[14] Another version of Ioannes is Jonah, Yod Vav Nun Hay. The text suggests that Jonah was not swallowed by the whale, but rather that he *was* the whale, or rather a version of the half man, half-Cetacean Oannes. In the Book of Jonah, chapter 1, verses 2 and 3, Jonah disregards the word of Yaweh (the 'Lord' in the English version) and insists on going down to the sea. This is a coded way of indicating that, as an amphibious mammal, he needs to get back to the water.

"We shall be seeking for traces of aeonial truth and a foundation of immutable things in these sacred numbers... for it is equally inconceivable that a book framed for the guidance and enlightenment of the whole human race should contain statements of an unintelligible nature, or to which the key has been permanently lost".[15] This statement can, I believe, be applied to the Hebrew text of the Old Testament.

2

THE CUBE OF LIGHT

Of all numbers Bond and Lea accord primacy to the number 8. However, they develop the seven rays in relation to the cube and show that, if each side of the cube is equal to 100, then the total length of the seven rays adds up to a number between 897 and 898. The first of these (897) is the gematria of the phrase in the Greek text of Revelation 1:4, "The seven churches which are in Asia" and the gematria of "the seven stars" is 898 "the seven stars or rays which are the angels of the seven churches".[1] In other words the seven rays are the spiritual energies which are given expression by the seven churches. In the Hebrew text these seven rays are manifested as the Pleiades, Kaf Yod Mem, whose gematria is 70 (7 × 10) and clearly the seven stars referred to in Revelation are the Pleiades. Their Hebrew name Chem is the root of our words chemistry and alchemy. In Greek mythology the Pleiades are the seven daughters of Atlas, "placed by Zeus among the stars". Only six of these stars are distinctly visible, suggesting a link with Bond and Lea's 'seventh light' that is only revealed when the hexagon is turned. This same effect is demonstrated in Figure 1, where what appears as a hexagon in two dimensions is revealed as a cube, with all 27 letters shown in their places. "And I turned to see the voice which spake with me. And having turned, I saw seven golden candle sticks".[2] It is not the viewer who is turned, however, but the cube, revealing that there are seven, not six, lights. Here 'voice', phonen in the Greek, is the accusative of phonē and has the gematria 1408, a key measure in Bond and Lea's Cabala of the Fish.[3] There are strong hints of a system based on three dimensions – arithmetic, geometric and musical – which originate in star systems such as the Pleiades and Sirius. There is further evidence of this nature in Bond and Lea's Cabala of the Fish, which we shall look at when we get to that part of the book.

"In the three incommensurable orders of magnitude derived from the measures of the cube" – that is, of the relative lengths of the rays in the diagram on page 27, 1, $\sqrt{2}$ and $\sqrt{3}$ — "we have clearly a very suggestive parallel to the...three kinds of light in the Lord's endyma [robe]". They then point out that the spectrum really consists of three colours, "and that the blending of these three produce the effect of seven" and this is perfectly reflected in the three kinds of ray, based on 1, $\sqrt{2}$ and $\sqrt{3}$ and the total of seven rays. The three primary colours are red, green and violet, the colours "of Jesus's three robes" according to the Pistis Sophia, and the gematria of endyma is 500, so that the three robes combined give the number 1500 and this is, as Bond and Lea point out, also the gematria of the Greek 'phōs' (light). They then show that, taking the wavelengths of light at the extremes of the visible spectrum, deep red and violet, and that of the mid point green, then the wavelength of red light is equal to that of green multiplied by $\sqrt{2}$ and that of violet is equal to that of red multiplied by $1/\sqrt{3}$. In other words the proportions shown in the cube of light and the wavelengths of the three primary colours are based on the same mathematical relationships.

In the Old Testament colour symbolism has a similar significance, but the colours are different and there are four of them: "And upon the skirts of [the robe of the High Priest] thou shalt make pomegranates of blue, and of purple, and of scarlet...and bells of gold between them".[4] Here again, as in the Pistis Sophia, we have the colours of a robe and 'robe' in Hebrew is Mem Ayn Yod Lammed, whose gematria is 150, which is equal to 1500/10, confirming the link with the Endymata of the Greek text.

However, since there are four colours, their underlying meaning cannot relate to the spectrum in the way that the endymata do. Looking through the text of the Old Testament for the occurrence of four related objects, we have the four creatures in Ezekiel, which had "the faces of a man, a lion, an ox and an eagle".[5] These suggest an astrological association: the second creature, Leo, the third Taurus and the fourth Scorpio. These are three of the four so-called fixed signs and the fourth of these is Aquarius, the water bearer, which is depicted as a man, hence Ezekiel's first creature. Solomon's magic ring had four jewels set in it, given to him by an angel, one in the shape of a whale, one of an eagle, one of a lion and the fourth of a serpent. These suggest variations of Ezekiel's creatures. As we shall see the constellation Taurus is associated with gravity and the massive size and weight of the whale also suggest this; the serpent is associated with the sign of Scorpio and the eagle, being a bird, suggests the air sign Aquarius.

In the Old Testament, in the second chapter of the Book of Numbers, is a description of what is referred to as the "Camp of the

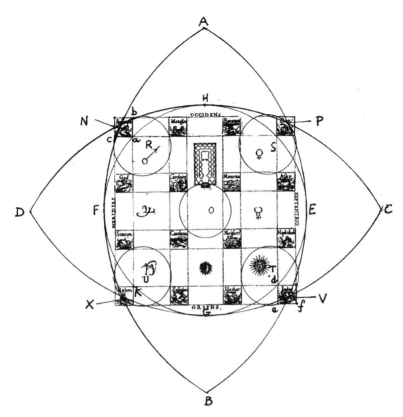

Figure 3. The four-petalled lotus and Villalpanda's Camp of the Israelites. In the four corner sites, those occupied by the tribes of Ephraim, Dan, Judah and Ruben, the inner circle with centre 0 and diameter EF marks the inner corners at a and d and the curves of the petals mark the corners at b and c, e and f.

Israelites". This describes the twelve tribes arranged around the perimeter of a square, oriented to the four main compass points. "And those that pitch on the east side . . . shall be they of the standard of the camp of Judah. . . . On the south side shall be the standard of the camp of Reuben . . . on the west side shall be the camp of Ephraim. . . . On the north side shall be the standard of the camp of Dan . . .".[6]

Figure 3 shows Villalpanda's diagram of the camp of the Israelites in Stirling's *The Canon*.[7] Villalpanda shows the tribes arranged around the perimeter of the camp, with the names of the corresponding constellations. These are identified in the Old Testament text as follows: "Judah is a lion's whelp",[8] "Ephraim is an heifer that loveth to tread the corn",[9] "Dan shall be a serpent in the way".[10] Hence Judah corresponds to the constellation of the lion, Ephraim to Taurus and Dan to Scorpio, with Reuben being Aquarius, the water-carrier, a 'man'.

But which colour is associated with each of the four tribes/signs? Leo is ruled by the sun astrologically and Judah is the royal house, so clearly its colour must be gold; the sign of the bull is an earth sign, suggesting the colour red ("like a red rag to a bull"), Scorpio is a water sign, hence blue, so that the remaining colour, purple, is that of Aquarius.

The arrangement of the squares in which the symbols are placed suggests that if the solution of the mystery (of the significance of the camp) is a geometrical one, it depends on the problem of squaring the circle (i.e. obtaining a square and a circle with the same area). The old method was to draw a circle with a diameter equal to eight and then to draw a square about the same centre, whose diagonal is equal to ten. In the Camp of the Israelites (Figure 3) the diagonal of each of the small squares in which each of the twelve tribes is contained, is equal to one-tenth of the diagonal of the large square, NPVX, NV (and PX). A circle is then drawn with centre 0 and a diameter of an O, so that its circumference passes through the inner corners of the squares containing the four corner tribes . . . this gives it the required diameter of 8 in relation to the square's diameter of 10 and square and circle have the same area. Figure 4 shows how this can be done geometrically. The arc AEB is drawn about the centre F, the arc AFB is drawn about the centre E, the arc CGD is drawn about H and the arc CHD is drawn about G. This gives the four-petalled lotus. "The four angels of the four quarters of Heaven . . . stand each on a lotus" (here on the four petals, at A, B, C and D).[11] They stand in higher dimensions and are expressed within our three-dimensional world within the square, whose corners, at N, P, V and X, are at the intersections of the lotus petals. To complete the figure, a circle with the same diameter as that of the arcs of the petals, but with its centre at that of the whole figure, is drawn, having the same area as that of the square.

In Figure 3, the diagram of the Camp of the Israelites, two other corners of the small squares of the corner tribes are determined by the arcs of the petals. For example, in the square of Ephraim/Taurus, one arc passes through the corner b, and another through the corner c. The geometrical method for squaring the circle is based on Bligh Bond's 74 foot squares on which he bases his plan of Glastonbury Abbey.[12] The sides of the square measure 74 feet, or 888 inches, the gematria of Jesus in Greek and the diameter of the circle of equal area is 88 feet, the gematria of Thoth and the lengths of the petals, AB and CD, are 153 feet, the fishes in the net in John 21.

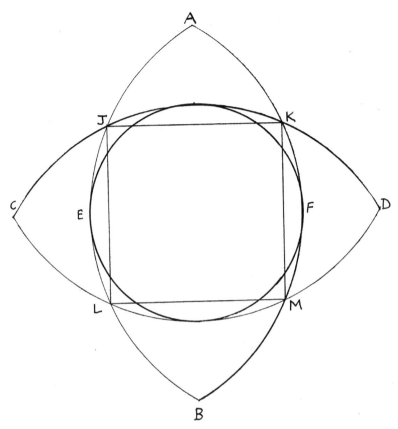

*Figure 4. The four-petalled Lotus at Glastonbury. AB and CD=153 feet;
EF=88 feet. The sides of the square JKLM=74 feet=888 inches. The area of
the square=740 square megalithic yards.*

The four jewels are those in Solomon's magic ring, which were in
the form of a whale, an eagle, a lion and a serpent.[13] The whale, by its
great size, suggests gravity. Weak nuclear force initates the transforma-
tion of elements in the stars, including our Sun, so it could be argued
that it corresponds to Leo rather than Aquarius.

The squaring of the circle reflects "the search for a gate, a key to the
passage from one world to another...".[14] The circles represent higher
dimensions and the squares are their physical, three-dimensional expression. It is the four fixed signs of Leo, Aquarius, Taurus and Scorpio that
embody the grounding of higher energies in our physical world and, out
of the twelve signs, they are the only ones which lie outside the central
circle. In terms of modern physics, they are the four fundamental

Figure 5. The New Jerusalem.

forces, on which physics is based – the forces of electromagnetism, strong nuclear force, weak nuclear force and gravity.

Figure 5 shows the "geometrical figure called the New Jerusalem in the apocalypse (the Book of Revelation)". Stirling states that the circumferences of the two circles which form the vesica piscis at the centre of the figure are "nearly 360",[15] but the Hebrew word for 'standard' used to refer to those at the corners of the camp of the Israelites is Nun Sheen Yod, whose gematria is 360, suggesting a link between the camp and the New Jerusalem. Stirling states that "It is well known that the four beasts which appear in the midst of the four wheels in Ezekiel's vision are identical with ... the devices upon the four standards of the Camp of the Israelites, where they stand for the four corner signs of the zodiac – Taurus, Leo, Scorpio and Aquarius". Given that the intersecting circles have circumferences of "nearly 360" (the "nearly" refers to the fact that we are dealing with the π ratio, which cannot be measured exactly, so we will call their circumference 360) and these circles determine the dimensions of the four corner squares, where the 'standards' are located, whose gematria in the Hebrew is 360.

Table 1. The four corners of the camp

Astrological sign	Tribe	Ezekiel's creature	Jewel	Colour	Element	Fundamental force
Taurus	Ephraim	Cherub	Whale	Red	Earth	Gravity
Aquarius	Reuben	Man	Eagle	Purple	Air	Weak nuclear force
Leo	Judah	Lion	Lion	Gold	Fire	Electro-magnetism
Scorpio	Dan	Serpent	Serpent	Blue	Water	Strong nuclear force

"And the city lieth foursquare, and he measured the wall thereof a hundred and forty and four cubits, according to the measure of a man, that is, of an angel".[16] While the circumference of the defining circles is 360, which equals 15×24, 144 equals 6×24. Furthermore, there are four of these small circles and $4 \times 144 = 576$, which is the gematria of the Greek word pneuma, meaning spirit, or breath, the creative energy whose physical expression is symbolised by the New Jerusalem and the Camp of the Israelites. In his description of the four creatures, Ezekiel states that they "had the likeness of a man"[17] and when John refers to "the measure of a man" he is linking his vision of the New Jerusalem to Ezekiel's vision. So, in the Old Testament, we have a description of a creative system based on the four fixed signs of astrology, the four fundamental forces of physics, giving rise to a four-square physical system, John's four-square city, while, in the Pistis Sophia we have the spectrum of light expressed in the cube of light and it is through light that the physical world is made visible to us. Table 1 shows all the correspondences between the astrological signs, tribes, elements etc.

"...ten curtains, of fine twined linen, and blue, and purple, and scarlet...the work of the cunning workman...".[18] This is repeated many times in the Book of Exodus, in connection with the furnishing of the Tabernacle and the design of the High Priest's clothes. In Hebrew 'twined linen' is Sheen Nun Yod Vav Sheen Sheen, the word Sheen Nun Yod meaning literally 'twinned', indicating that the 'thread' which is being woven into the 'curtains' consists of two strands. This is the creative energy, which polarises as it enters the third dimension and forms our whole physical world, symbolised here by the colours. This word Sheen Nun Yod is an anagram of Nun Sheen Yod, the standards at the four corners of the Camp and therefore has

11

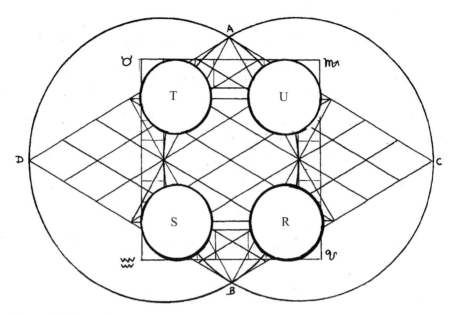

Figure 6. Solomon's magic ring, with its four jewels at R, S, T and U and his magic carpet, the rhombus ABCD. The jewels correspond to the four fixed astrological signs, Leo, Aquarius, Taurus and Scorpio.

the same gematria, 360, another link with the two circles which form the basis of the New Jerusalem.

The second of these two words, Vav Sheen Sheen, is translated as linen, or cotton, but essentially it refers to any woven material. Without the prefix Vav, it has the gematria 600, which is equal to 25×24, while $360 = 15 \times 24$. 600 is also the gematria of ē theotēs, the Godhead, "the Divine counterpart of kosmos",[19] whose gematria is also 600. The four circles with centres R, S, T and U, one within each corner of the Camp of the lsraelites in Figure 6, represent the settings of the four jewels of Solomon's magic ring, Ezekiel's four creatures etc. Their circumference is equal to 360/2.5, where 360 is the circumference of the large circles and $360/2.5 = 144$. "And the city lieth foursquare... and he measured the wall thereof, a hundred and forty and four cubits".[20] This puts all the aspects of Table 1 firmly within the proportions based on the circles whose circumference is 360 in the Camp of the Israelites. The centre circle, whose circumference is also 144, is the inner ring in Bond and Lea's Metacubon[21] and is the gematria of Abram (Abraham), whose seed shall be "as the stars of the heaven and as the sand which is upon the sea shore".[22] This reveals Abraham as a cosmic creative being, just as are the twelve 'tribes' as shown in the Camp of the Israelites. We have here both a description of a system of creative energies and the means by which they are expressed in our three-dimensional world, through the four fundamental forces. All this confirms that the Book of Exodus is not merely a tribal history, but is an account of the cosmic creative process, of which the Tabernacle and Solomon's Temple are expressions.

The expression 'cunning workman' is repeatedly associated with the building of the Tabernacle and with the four colours and, in the Hebrew text, these two words both have the same root of Hhayt Sheen, whose gematria is 308. The length of the Egyptian temple at Luxor is 308 megalithic yards (1 MY = 0.829 metres). Schwaller de Lubicz[23] shows that the distance from the "Axis of Measures", which is incised into the stones beneath the paving of the floor of the Covered Temple, the inner part of the building, to the west corner, is 22 MY (18.26 m) and this is equal to 20 English yards or 60 feet. The total length of the temple divided by 22, 308/22 = 14, a hint of the π ratio of 22/7 and perhaps a reference to the interlocking circles that form the basis of the temple plan. This gives a hint of the way in which the great temple-building initiates worked: "And King Solomon sent and fetched Hiram out of Tyre ... He was filled with wisdom and understanding and cunning ...".[24] The gematria of the root of this key word 'cunning', 308, links the Mosaic Tabernacle and Solomon's temple to the Ancient Egyptian tradition and reveals all these sacred structures as expressions of the cosmic creative process,

In reviewing the implications of the relative wavelengths of the red, green and violet rays and their arithmetical relationships based on $\sqrt{2}$ and $\sqrt{3}$, which Bond and Lea refer to as "those mysterious entities ... pointing to a genesis of motion in a region of space unknown to us",[25] we need to look again at the AlephBaytic cube which contains the Hebrew letters and the way in which the key combinations of letters in the Hebrew text operate within it. "... the Lord hath called by name Bezalel ... of the tribe of Judah ... and he hath filled him with the spirit of God and all manner of workmanship, ... to work in all manner of cunning workmanship ... that he may teach both he, and Aholiab ... of the tribe of Dan ... them hath he filled with wisdom of heart ... and of the cunning workman and of the embroiderer in blue and in purple and in scarlet and in fine linen, and of the weaver, ... and of those that devise cunning works".[26]

The first thing to notice about this passage is the repeated reference to 'cunning workmanship' and 'cunning works', which suggests that we

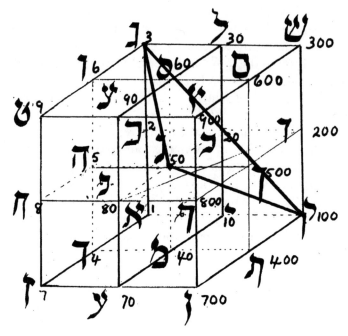

Figure 7. One hundred, fifty and three in the AlephBaytic cube. Three to one hundred, a diagonal on the rear face of the cube. Three to fifty and one hundred to fifty, each $1 \times \sqrt{3/2}$ where $1 = $ length of one side.

are dealing with the creative process. Notice also that the text draws attention to the fact that Bezalel is "of the tribe of Judah", while Aholiab is "of the tribe of Dan". These two tribes are at corners of the Camp of the Israelites, hinting at the operation of the fundamental forces in the process of physical creation, in this case the building of the Tabernacle. In the case of Bezalel, Bayt Tsadde Lammed Aleph Lammed, the gematria is 153, written in John's Gospel as "one hundred, fifty and three".[27] The links between these three numbers are shown in Figure 7. Their positions in the cube demonstrate that they constitute a hologram of the cube, i.e. they provide the minimum information to enable it to be constructed, the centre and two corners. When Jesus stands on the shore and directs Peter and the six disciples to "cast the net on the other side", he is giving a demonstration of the creative process, in which the 'fish', the unformed energy, is 'caught', i.e. becomes crystallised within the 'net', or lattice. The lattice of the AlephBaytic cube is a three-dimensional version of the disciples' net. The gematria of Bezalel' partner's name, Aholiab, is 49, 7^2, an approximation of the diagonal of a 5×5 square, a reference to one of the sides of the square.

14

If we look at the eight cubic modules that make up the whole cube and make each side of these modules equal to 1, then the internal diagonal; the longest straight line which can be drawn within the cube, will be equal to $1 \times \sqrt{3}$. Such diagonals are formed by the gematria of Bezalel, "one hundred, fifty and three" the centre and the two corners of the large cube. In addition, the gematria of Bezalel's partner in building the Tabernacle, Aholiab, is 49, an approximation to the diagonal of a square whose sides have a length of 5, the diagonals of the faces of the cubes being equal to $1 \times \sqrt{2}$. Here we have these "mysterious entities" the roots of two and three, engaged in the genesis of three-dimensional form symbolised by the AlephBaytic cube. In being "filled with the spirit of God and all manner of workmanship", the writers are indicating that Bezalel and Aholiab understand how to work with these "mysterious entities" to carry out the process of physical creation. In Jewish mythology it is said that Bezalel knew how to use words as instruments of power and we can now see how he was able to do this.

3

THE METACUBES

As we saw, the first cube, the "Cube of One", determines the proportions of the settings for the jewels of Solomon's magic ring (see Figure 6). "...the second, which is the Cube of Two, exhibits Nineteen points".[1] This is the $2 \times 2 \times 2$ AlephBaytic cube, which has a total of 27 points, 19 of which are visible in a solid cube (see Figure 1). This suggests the 19 laevorotatory amino acids, those which produce a left-handed deflection of light in a spectroscope. The one remaining amino acid has no optical centre and this corresponds to the point at the centre of the cube, sometimes giving a left-handed and sometimes a right-handed rotation to light in the spectroscope. Amino acids are the components of all proteins and so here we have a hint of the part played by the AlephBaytic cube in mediating the creative energies expressed by the 27 letters of the Hebrew AlephBayt. The word nineteen in Hebrew is Tav Sheen Ayn Hay-Ayan Sheen Raysh, whose gematria is 1345 and $37 + 19 \times 24 = 1344$, the gematria of "The Way of the Lord" in Greek. Here we have Bond and Lea's second and third Metacubes combined in the gematria of the Hebrew word for 19, 19 and 37 being the visible points in the respective solid cubes with totals of 27 and 37 points, indicating the physical manifestation of the creative energies embodied in the cubes. The indication that we may be dealing with amino acids suggests that the manifestation may be in the form of living organisms.

Bligh Bond and Lea are mainly concerned with the occurrence of 37 and its multiples in the Greek "Names, Titles, or Epithets of Our Lord" in the New Testament and give large numbers of examples of these in their Appendix C. However, what I would claim is that a significant number of words and phrases with gematria of multiples of 37 also occur in the Hebrew text of the Old Testament. These extend far beyond the limits of any religious or dogmatic nature and are, I believe, truly universal.

"...and (Eve) conceived, and bare Cain...and again she bare Abel".[2] In the Hebrew text Abel is written as Hay Bayt lammed, whose gematria is 37, suggesting that Abel is a fundamental player in the creative process and especially in the evolution of Man, being a son of Adam and Eve. This is confirmed by the phrase "Abel was a keeper (of sheep)", where the gematria of the Hebrew is 312 ($= 13 \times 24$), which is the gematria of the Greek 'dēlos', meaning manifestation and 'āggelos', higher energies suggesting that Abel in the manifestation of the latter. The gematria of Abel, 37, is the number of visible points in the 3 cube, indicating physical manifestation.

". . . The voice of thy brother's blood crieth out to me from the ground." Suares is surely right in stating "Of course Cain had not killed (Abel)",[3] although one may not agree with his alternative explanation. However, the gematria of key words in this passage confirm that it is concerned with the cosmic creative process. 'Of blood' is Dallet Mem Yod, whose gematria is 54 and 'brother' Aleph Hhayt Yod, is 19, the visible points of the Cube of Two and $54 + 19 = 63$ while the Cube of Three has 64 points, indicating that Abel is concerned with the hidden part of the cube (27 points being on the hidden sides of the solid cube, with 37 on the visible sides and $37 + 27 = 64$, the total points in the Cube of Three), i.e. with the creative energies in higher dimensions.

The shedding of his blood suggests the descent of creative energy into the third dimension and "from the ground" is Mem Final Nun-Hay Aleph Dallet Mem Hay, whose gematria is 55 and 740, where 55 refers back to the creative energy symbolised by Abel's blood and $740 = 37 \times 20$, the gematria of the Greek word 'ktisis', meaning 'creation', underlining the fact that we are dealing with the creative process.

We come now to a different aspect of the significance of the number 37. ". . . and they shall be given unto his hand until a time, and times and half a time".[4] This extraordinary statement is repeated in Daniel 12:7 and again in Revelation 12:14. The fact of its repetition indicates its importance but, as it stands, it is difficult to make any sense of it. However, half a time, time and times suggest proportions of 1, 2 and 4, perhaps two octaves in music, where the frequency range of each octave is double that of the octave below. If we then look at the Hebrew word for 'time', its root is Ayn Dallet, whose gematria is 74 and the note D two octaves below middle C has a frequency of 74 Hz, confirming the musical link. We now have the following:

	Half a time	Time	Times
Notes	D_1	D	D
	37 Hz	74 Hz	148 Hz

This also suggests the musical significance of the number 37, and points to the harmonic basis of the whole Hebrew text of the Old Testament. It also indicates that the gematria is a key to an understanding of the harmonic nature of the creative process. All this fits with Bond and Lea's Cube of Light and the relationships between the wavelengths/frequencies of the three rays.[5] In Vedic myth, the note D is the 'linchpin' of Indra's chariot wheel. The "linchpin on D represents the reference tone around which the tone field unfolds".[6] McClain is describing the creative symbolism behind the musical aspects of Vedic myth. This amplifies the musical aspects of the creative process revealed by gematria in the Hebrew text.

Another example of a significant word whose gematria is a multiple of 37 is the Greek 'Christos' (Christ), whose gematria is 1480 ($= 37 \times 40$).[7] "Priest of Midian"[8] has the gematria 1479 and this 'priest' was Moses' father-in-law – Moses 'married' one of Jethro's seven 'daughters', who were, in fact seven occult sciences taught to Moses by the initiate Jethro/Ruel.[9] Perhaps one of those seven was the science of gematria. All this puts Jesus Christ firmly into the Mosaic tradition, making it clear that Jesus's message is universal and inclusive, rather than narrowly dogmatic and exclusive, in the way that orthodox Christianity tries to present it.

One of the key numbers in Bond and Lea's thesis is 888, which is equal to 37×24, the gematria of Jesus written in Greek. In the Metacubes, this consists of all the visible points of the Cube of Four. Jesus Christ, on the other hand, has the gematria of 2368, which is equal to 37×64, where 64 is the total number of points in the Cube of Four, including the 27 points on the three hidden sides. "And Jesus, when he was baptised, saw the spirit of God descending, as a dove, and coming upon him".[10] The Greek word for dove is 'peristera', whose gematria is 901 and the gematria of 'apsinthos' (wormwood) is 900. The reader may say "So what?" After all there is no link between a dove and the bitter herb wormwood. However, the following passage from Revelation suggests otherwise: ". . . and there fell from heaven a great star . . . and the name of the star is called Wormwood".[11] Both these events, the descent of the dove, symbolising the descent of the Christos into the physical vehicle Jesus, and the descent of the great star, describe the coming down of immense energies from higher dimensions, one being what we would call positive, the other negative. It is their immensity and the fact that they are descending 'from above' that concerns us here and the linking of the two apparently unconnected events through the gematria that reveals the cosmic nature of the incarnation of the Christ in the earthly being of Jesus. The gematria of 'Christos' is 1480 and, added to that of Jesus, 1480 + 888, gives 2368, or 64 × 24, the complete Cube of Four, in which the hidden three sides represents the Christ, while the three visible sides (37 × 24 = 888) represent Jesus.

In Genesis chapter 28, after his dream, Jacob takes the stone that had been his pillow and erects it as a pillar (omphalos, or standing stone) ...and he called the name of that place Beth-el. "Truly this is...the house of God..." and Bethel is Bayt Yod Tav-Aleph Lammed, whose gematria is 443, while 444 × 2 = 888, Jesus. Beth-el literally means 'House of God' and, in taking the stone on which he had laid his head while dreaming, and setting it up as omphalos, whose gematria is 911 (912 = 38 × 24, literally 'world navel'), Jacob is establishing the link between World Teacher and sacred place, temple etc. "Jesus said... Destroy this temple, and in three days I will raise it up.... He spake of the temple of his body".[12] In the Greek this temple is 'ton naon', whose gematria is 591 and 592 = 37 × 16, the gematria of the Greek 'Theotes' (Godhead), confirming the link between The Christ's body and the 'House of God'.

Just as 888 is the number of visible points in the Cube of Four, each counted as 24, so 456 is the number of visible points in the Cube of Two, when each is likewise counted as 24 and the gematria of 'mēter' (mother in Greek) is 456.[13] The root of this word 'mēter' is Maat, or Maēt, the name of the Egyptian Goddess of measure and the origin of the English word 'mete', as in 'to mete out'. Written in Hebrew it is Mem Hhayt, whose gematria is 48 and 49 (Hebrew mem Zayn Bayt − altar = 49) is approximately the length of the diagonal of a 5 × 5 square, hence defining or measuring the faces of the Cubes.It is also the origin of the Latin word matrix (womb) and the English 'woman' is an abbreviation of 'womb-man', bearer of the womb. In Hebrew woman is Aleph Sheen Hay, whose gematria is 306 and 306/2 = 153, the fishes in the net in John 21. The 'catching of the fishes' (free energy) in the 'net' (the crystal lattice) is an allegory for the process of physical creation. In John's account Jesus stands on the shore, demonstrating this alchemical process. A similar process takes place during gestation in the womb, as the embryo develops.

Twice 888, the number of Jesus, is 1776, the gematria when written in Greek, of the phrase The Saviour of Israel. In the Greek text of the Septuagint we have 'os tous asteras', translated "as it were the stars"[14] whose gematria is also 1776. We have here an account of Abram's founding of Israel. Abram was not born at some place called "Ur of the Chaldees", but was an initiate, a member of the Awr Kasdeem, magicians of light. "According to the esoteric tradition, Abram was the first really to understand the deep significance" of the statement that "the sons of Elohim came in unto the daughters of men, and they bare children to them".[15] Therefore Abram's children are children of the Gods. It is hardly surprising that Yaweh drove Adam and Eve out of Eden, thereby blanking out their memory of their (and our) memory of our divine inheritance. "And Yaweh said, behold the man is become as one of us...".[16]

"And the angel of Yaweh called unto Abram.... In blessing I will bless thee...".[17] and 'blessing' is Bayt Dallet Final Khaf, whose gematria is 702, while the gematria of 'The God of Israel' is 703, which is equal to 37×19 and 19 is the number of visible points in the Cube of Two, the Cube of the Mother, the latter being a reference to the "daughters of men" who bare children unto the Gods (the Elohim).[18] Verse 17 continues: "and in multiplying I will multiply thy seed... and thy seed shall possess the gate of his enemies". In the Hebrew the gematria of 'seed' is 777 (37×21). This is the gematria of the Greek 'stauros', the Cross.[19] The repetition of 'seed' gives the gematria $2 \times 777 = 1554 = 37 \times 42$ and this is the gematria of the Greek 'anastasis sarkos', the resurrection of the body.

"And Absalom rode upon his mule... under the thick boughs of a great oak, and his head caught hold of the oak, and he was taken up between the heaven and the earth.... And (Joab) took three darts in his hand and thrust them through the heart of Absalom, while he yet alive...".[20] In Egyptian mythology Osiris is murdered by his brother Set, who puts the body into a chest and throws it into the sea. It is washed up at Byblos, at the foot of a tamarisk tree which "grew to enclose it". The tree is then cut down and eventually Osiris's body is released and restored to life. Hence Osiris is essentially the tree, or tree god, symbolising the cycle of birth, death and resurrection.

Absalom "caught up in the great oak" represents the same Osirian tradition of birth, death and resurrection and, as the founding father, Abram sets this cycle in motion, as suggested by the repetition of 'seed', with its gematria of 1554, 'anastasis sarkos', resurrection of the body. The name 'Absalom' is correctly AbSalmon, where 'Salmon' is a title like 'Pharoah'. (Solomon is another form of the title 'Salmon'.) David's son usually referred to as 'Solomon' had the given name Jedidiah.[21]

In the account of Jesus's crucifixion in John 19:34, one of the soldiers with a spear pierced Jesus's side, surely an indication that Jesus was in the same Osirian tradition of the tree deity embodying the cycle of birth, death and resurrection as in Joab's action in piercing Absalom with the three darts. In the Hebrew text of 2 Samuel 18:14, 'three darts' has the gematria 1556 and 1554 is the gematria of the Greek 'anastasis sarkos', resurrection of the body, confirming that the account of Absalom hanging in the tree is a reference to the Osirian tradition of the tree deity and the life cycle.

Bond and Lea discuss the significance of the gematria of the name Ioannes (John) in the context of two other words, Baptisma and Ieou.[22] The first of these has the gematria 1119, the same as Ioannes. The second of these, Ieou is referred to in the Gnostic books as the 'Bishop of Light'. In Hebrew it is Aleph Hay Yod Hay (translated into Engish as 'I am'). This name "is derived from a much earlier and very ancient name of God, an old name of the supreme deity of the Shemites ('Shem' indicating initiates). This Being represented the Spiritual Light Principle".[23] The gematria of Ieou is 485, while that of the Hebrew Aleph Hay Yod Hay is 21 and $21 \times 23 = 483$, confirming that they both refer to the same Being.

Bond and Lea show an equilateral triangle contained within a square whose sides have the same length.[24] My Figure 8 shows the same triangle within a square, but with different measurements. The sides of the square EFGH and the triangle AEF have a length of 90, while AO is 80 long, so that the ratio AO:AE is 8:9, that of the major whole tone in music, for example, an open pipe, such as an organ pipe, which is two feet long, will give the note middle c, while one whose length is 1 foot 9 inches will give the note d, the ratio 2 feet to 1 foot 9 inches being 9:8. We saw the significance of the note d in relation to the harmonic basis of the Hebrew text. Here we have the transition from the higher vibrational level suggested by the triangle (an intermediary between the highest level indicated by the circle or sphere and the dense physical indicated by the square EFGH).

Figure 12 shows Bond and Lea's triangle and square in the context of the whole Cosmic Scheme, where the corners G and H lie on the overlapping outer circles (infinity), the creative energies entering the triangle at A, flowing down its sides to E and F and out into the square, the physical world.

With Bond and Lea's triangle divided in half to form AEO and AFO, in addition to a fundamental musical proportion, the major whole-tone of 8:9, we have a geometric proportion of equal significance: the ratio EO:AO is $1:\sqrt{3}$, so that:

where EO $= 45$, $\sqrt{3} \times 45 = 78$.

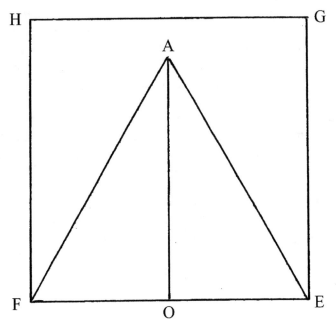

Figure 8. An equilateral triangle drawn within a square. The square EFGH and the equilateral triangle AEF drawn within it have sides with a length of 90. In mathematical terms, the half base EO × 3 = AO, and where EO=45, AO=78. In musical terms, if AO=80, then AE – 90, a ratio of 8:9, that of the major wholetone in music. Thus the equilateral triangle combines, in its proportions, those of mathematics and music.

But, as we know, when based on musical proportion, AO = 80 and the arithmetical proportion gives, in musical terms, a slight flattening. In dealing with irrational numbers, such as $\sqrt{3}$ exact measures cannot be obtained, but the two figures 80 and 78 are remarkably close.

Looking again at Figure 7, showing the gematria of Bezalel "one hundred, fifty and three", drawn within the AlephBaytic cube each line from the centre (50) to the two corners of the cube (3 and 100), makes a diagonal within one of the eight cubic modules which make up the whole cube, the longest straight line that can be drawn within the cube. Then, if the length of each side is equal to 1, the length of these diagonals is $1 \times \sqrt{3} = 1.73$, the dimension that turns a two-dimensional hexagon into a three-dimensional cube. This is a fundamental aspect of the holographic nature of the three points, 100, 50 and 3.

This ratio of $1:\sqrt{3}$ is common to all the vesicas and their contained rhombuses (ABCD, ABEF and the small vesica with long axis EF).

22

Written in Greek, the names of the three gods, Hermes, Zeus and Apollo have the gematria respectively of 353, 612 and 1061 a $\sqrt{3}$ series, in which $\sqrt{3} \times 353 = 612$ and $\sqrt{3} \times 612 = 1061$. As with the descending hierarchy of energies expressed by the large circles with centres E and F, the triangle AEF and the square EFGH, here we have a similar hierarchy expressed geometrically by the interlocking vesicas, with the names of the three 'gods' providing a mathematical clue to the geometry and the hierarchy of energies which are expressed by the Cosmic Scheme. Since EF ($= 353$, Hermes), the lowest number in this series based on $\sqrt{3}$, is also the length of the sides of the square EFGH, the latter symbolises the physical expression of these higher energies.

Bond and Lea look at creative sound, expressed by the voice in words.[25] In Hebrew 'the word of the Gods', or 'The Sons of God', is Dallet Bayt Raish Aleph Lammed Hay Yod Final Mem, whose gematria is 852 and $851 = 37 \times 23$ and is the gematria of the Greek word 'yparksis', meaning 'substance' and it is exactly The Word of God which gives physical substance to the higher creative energies.

The Hebrew word Dallet Bayt Raysh, meaning word, is very similar to Dallet Bayt Yod Raish, the Holy of Holies in the Temple, the oracular space in which the word of God is pronounced to the High Priest and while the Greek word 'logos' (word) has the gematria 373, the Hebrew word for the Holy of Holies, the Dbir, has the gematria 216 and $216 \times \sqrt{3} = 373$, a remarkable link between the Greek for word and the Hebrew for the cubic space in which that word is pronounced. The way that $\sqrt{3}$ links the cubic oracular space of the Debir with the Word, the oracular pronouncement, is emphasised by the fact that the internal diagonal of the cubic space is expressed as the length of its sides multiplied by $\sqrt{3}$ and it is not by chance that the letters of the Hebrew AlephBayt are contained in a cubic space. The seven strings of Apollo's lute were connected with the seven vowels of the Greek alphabet and these were run together in one breath, as the "mystical and unspeakable name of God".[26] As we know this name is written in the Hebrew as Aleph Hay Yod Hay and in the Greek as Iao. It is in the Debir, or Holy of Holies, the cubic oracular space in the inner Temple, that the God speaks. This creative energy expressed in sound, Bond and Lea's 'phonē', sets up three-dimensional resonant patterns, as is demonstrated in Figure 2. Figure 9 shows the sacred Hebrew name of God, Aleph Hay Yod Hay, drawn in the AlephBaytic cube. Both these lines; from Aleph to Hay (1 to 5) and from Yod to Hay (10 to 5), lie in the lower rear cubic module, one of the eight making up the whole cube. Making the length of each edge in these modules equal to 1, then the

אהיה

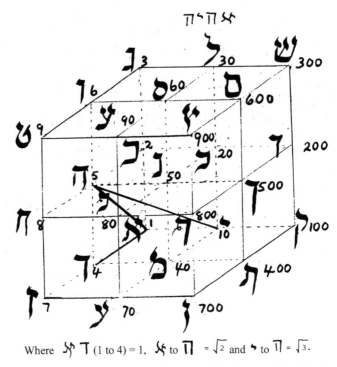

Where אלף ד (1 to 4) = 1, א to ה = $\sqrt{2}$ and י to ה = $\sqrt{3}$.

Figure 9. Aleph Hay Yod Hay, the Sacred Name of God, in the AlephBaytic cube. Hence the aeonial nature of the Sacred name is revealed within the AlephBaytic cube.

line from Aleph to Hay forms a diagonal across the face of this module, whose length is $1 \times \sqrt{2}$ and the line from Yod to Hay forms an internal diagonal within this cube whose length is $1 \times \sqrt{3}$. Here we have a perfect example in which the sounding of the sacred name of God, Aleph Hay Yod Hay, within the cubic space of the Debir, the oracle as it is often translated (e.g. 1 Kings 8:5) manifests the second dimension (Aleph to Hay), and the third dimension (Yod Hay), a demonstration of the descent of the higher creative energies to create our physical world. In the Greek tradition, in the oracle centre at Delphi, this creative energy is embodied in the Python, a serpent, just as it is in the Hebrew version of the myth of creation contained in the story of Adam and Eve in the Garden of Eden.[27] This role played by the serpent is confirmed by the term pneuma pythonos, 'a spirit of divination'. Its gematria is 2185 and $2183 = 37 \times 59$, the gematria, written in Greek, of "Head over all to the Church".[28] Furthermore, the gematria of 'āggelos', meaning 'messenger', but usually translated as 'angel', is 312 and $312 \times 7 = 2184$. These are the creative energies flowing up and down the ladder in Jacobs's dream.[29] The 7 suggests the octave in music, perhaps seven 'rungs' on the ladder, the hierarchy of frequency levels extending up to infinity. It is this flow of creative energy which is controlled and manipulated by the deity associated with the oracle centre, for example Apollo at Delphi and Delos, within the cubic space, speaking the appropriate words to create the desired physical form. The Hebrew myth which states that Bezalel "knew how to use letters as instruments of power" means exactly this.

"And Jacob rose up early in the morning, and took the stone that he had put under his head, and set it up for a pillar . . . and he called the name of that place Beth-el, that is The House of God".[30] In Greek 'pillar' is written as 'omphalos', meaning 'world navel', where 'navel' indicates a point at which energy enters a body, in this case the Earth. The gematria of navel is 911 and $912/2 = 456$, the gematria of 'mother', hence the navel as the point at which mother and child (Deity and planet) are linked.

In referring to the place where he had placed the omphalos as "the House of God", Jacob makes the link between the oracle centre and the navel stone. The gematria of Beth-el written in Hebrew is 443 and $444 = 37 \times 12$. 444 is also the gematria of Qof Dallet Sheen-Lammed Yod, translated as "sanctify unto me" and, in raising the pillar, Jacob was indeed sanctifying the place to the deity. Omphaloi are frequently associated with sacred places in the Egyptian, Hebrew and Greek traditions. Temple[31] refers to an omphalos stone "found by Reisner in the great temple of Amon at Thebes in Egypt. This stone was placed in the main room of the temple where the meridian and parallel actually cross". Temple shows the plan of the ancient Egyptian geodetic schema – the Eastern Axis of this schema passes through the temple at Thebes at longitude 32 degrees 38 minutes East and at latitude 25 degrees 42 minutes North. This suggests that the whole landscape is set out as a result of energy patterns put together by the deity, in this case Amon, within the House of God, the oracular cube. The Great Pyramid can be regarded as an enormous omphalos, "whose object was the fertilisation of the Egyptian plain, perhaps of an even larger area".[32] This statement is applicable to the part played by omphaloi and oracle centres in general. The maintenance of the Earth and all its creatures in a state of health and harmony was dependent on the manipulation of the higher creative energies coming into the oracle centres and their direction out into the surrounding areas.

Godfrey Higgins[33] connects the sacred syllable OM with Delphi, which he says is "not far from the divina vox of the Greeks", which is none other than Bond and Lea's 'phonē', "the Voice or Sound that brings the Worlds into manifestation".[34] It is the Creative Sound AUM of Eastern tradition and of the Sacred Name of God, Aleph Hay Yod Hay in the Hebrew. Hesychius "interprets the word OMPH (as in omphalos) to be theia chledon, the sacred voice, the holy sound"[35] and hence the omphalos is the place where this creative sound is made. The gematria of theia chladon is 1517 ($= 37 \times 41$) and this is also the gematria of 'ē archē kosmos', 'the beginning of the cosmos', confirming the link with the creative process.

Bond and Lea build up, through the gematria of a series of words and phrases from the Greek text, to the phrase "Priest after the order of Melchisedek",[36] whose gematria written in Greek is 2740, while $2738 = 37 \times 37 + 37$. The Hebrew form of Melchisedek is written as Mem Lammed Kaf Yod-Tsadde Dallet Qof, literally 'King-Priest' (Malech-Zedek)/Zedek referring to an order of king-priests. "The Greek word for Messiah is 'Christ' or 'Christos'. The term – whether in Hebrew or Greek – meant simply 'the anointed one' and generally referred to a king. Thus David, when he was anointed king ... became, quite explicitly, a 'Messiah' or a 'Christ'. And every subsequent Jewish king of the house of David was known by the same appellation".[37] Hence the 'order of Melchisedek' refers to this line of king-priests, extending from David, of which Jesus Christ was the heir. Just as 'Solomon and 'Absalom' are versions of the title 'the Salmon', so 'Melchizedek' is the title of an order of king-priests.

In the passage from Zecharia 3:1, "And he showed me Joshua the High Priest", for 'High Priest' the Hebrew has Hay Kaf Hay Final Nun Hay Gimmel Dallet Vav Lammed, whose gematria is 778 and $777 = 37 \times 21$, the gematria of the Greek 'stauros', the cross. As we saw, this links up with the Osirian tree-deity tradition, in which the Salmon (Solomon, Absalom), is sacrificed in a tree, or on a cross. Perhaps the Melchisedek order emphasises the priestly aspect, while that of the Salmon is more concerned with the kingly role.

Bond and Lea state that "... all these numbers (revealed by the gematria of the Hebrew or Greek texts) are of one order and can be expressed as a mathematical or algebraical series representative of fundamental principles in the geometry of the Aeons".[38] We now know that this expression is given three-dimensional form within the AlephBaytic Cube – the $2 \times 2 \times 2$ cube in Bond and Lea's Metacube. Figure 10 shows the AlephBaytic cube within the aeonial Geometry of the Cosmic Scheme. The Word, through its gematria, forms the basis for a

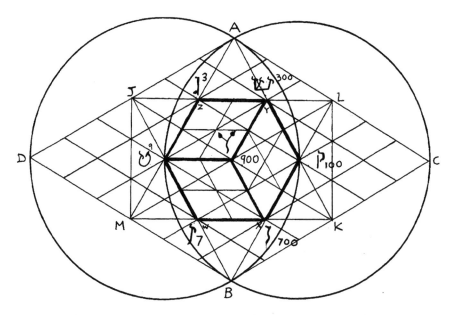

Figure 10. The AlephBaytic cube in the context of the Cosmic Scheme, showing how the positions of the letters within the cube are dictated by the musical proportions within the rectangle JKLM.

three-dimensional pattern and this pattern corresponds to the locations of atoms within the lattice of a particular crystal. "It is concerned with the successive operation of the Generative Power of the number Three..." and the authors then use, as an example, an equilateral triangle whose sides are equal to 1000. In Figure 11 we have a similar triangle whose sides are equal to 90 and we know that the ratio of its half base to its height $\sqrt{3} \times 45 = 78$, while, in musical terms, if the ratio of the length of the side to the height is 90:80, this gives the ratio 8:9, that of the major wholetone in music (for example the notes C and D). Since the discrepancy of 2 between 78 and 80 is less than 3% and only involves a slight flattening of the lower note, it seems quite acceptable musically and demonstrates the synthesis of the geometry and music in the creative process.

Bond and Lea then add the lengths of the three sides of the equilateral triangle together and subtract $\sqrt{3}$. If we do the same with the triangle of sides equal to 9 we get $3 \times 9 = 27 - 8 = 19$, where 27, 8 and 19 are respectively the total number of points in the AlephBaytic Cube, the number of points on the hidden sides of the cube and the

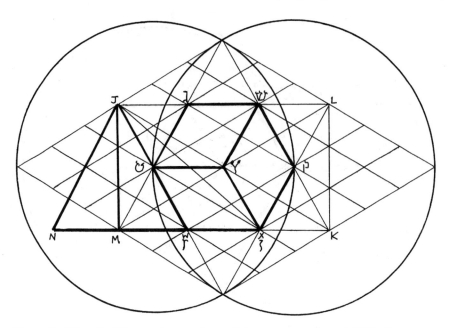

*Figure 11. The AlephBaytic cube and the musical proportions. JM=8, JW=9,
MW=4.5 giving the length of the sides of the cube.*

points on the visible sides. In Figure 11 the AlephBaytic Cube is shown in
the context of the aeonial geometry of the Cosmic Scheme. The musical
proportions are shown, so that if; for example, JM=8, Jw=9; the
proportion of the major wholetone and the distance Jx=12, so that the
ratio JM:Jx=2:3, the proportion of the musical fifth and the ratio
JM:JK=1:2 that of the octave, the diagram shows how the musical
proportions pick out the locations of letters in the cube. The remaining
proportions of the octave, thirds, fourths etc. locate the other letters
within the cube. "Cadmus sailed with Telephassa to Rhodes where
he...built Poseidon's temple, leaving a hereditary priesthood to care
for it" and to perform therapeutic music there".[39] No doubt Cadmus
ensured that, like all sacred buildings, its proportions conformed to
those in Figure 12. Using the measurements of Bond and Lea's
square,[40] the sides have a length of 33.5 and gematria of Kadmos is
335, suggesting that the temple which Kadmos dedicated to Poseidon
embodied proportions based on the gematria of his name. Furthermore,
the length of the vesica ABEF in Figure 12, showing the square and
equilateral triangle in the Cosmic Scheme, is 1219, the gematria of
Poseidon. The sides of the square, 335 and the length of the vesica/

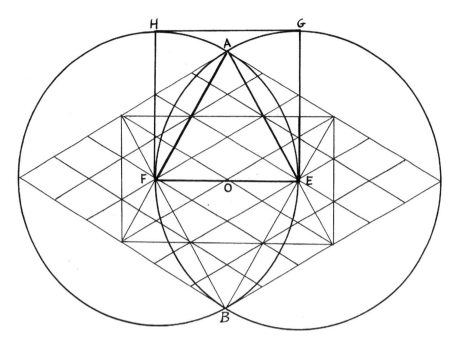

Figure 12. The square EFGH and equilateral triangle AEF, with common side EF, drawn within the Cosmic Scheme.

rhombus ABEF, together form a hologram for the construction of the whole building.

4

NUMBER

Here, Bond and Lea develop the idea of formative numbers and present the first seven of these: 7, 13, 19, 25, 31, 37 and 43.[1] They do not remark on the fact that one of these, 37, is the base number for their gematric series, and we have seen its significance in relation to the musical series based on the phrase "time, times and half a time (Daniel 12:7 etc.), where it suggests the frequency of the note D three octaves below middle C.

The first comment on this series of numbers is that they are all prime numbers (except 25) which suggests that these numbers, which are only divisible by themselves and 1, may be, by their nature, formative, i.e. fundamental in some way to the creative process.

Figure 13 shows the numbers up to 48 arranged in what appear as two concentric rings. Contrary to the conventional view, these numbers are not distributed randomly, but occur at regular intervals. In addition, they are all separated by numbers which are divisible by either 3 or 2, 16 of each. Those divisible by 3 are shown in Figure 14.[2] This insight into the nature of number seems to me to open up a new world and to merit another look at what Bond and Lea have to say. "...however remarkable the arithmetic correspondence shown (by the gematria), it would be of inferior importance unless the numbers themselves had some intrinsic meaning derived from their essential nature".[3] The pattern revealed in the numbers up to 48 gives a hint of what that meaning might be. Quoting Peter Plichta again: "I prepared a drawing in which I joined all numbers on the first circle to the centre. The result had – even visually – an astonishing similarity with the atomic model: a minute nucleus of conspicuously small size in relation to the giant surrounding shells".

Looking again at Plichta's drawing of the two concentric rings of numbers up to 48, Bond and Lea's Numbers of Perfection show that,

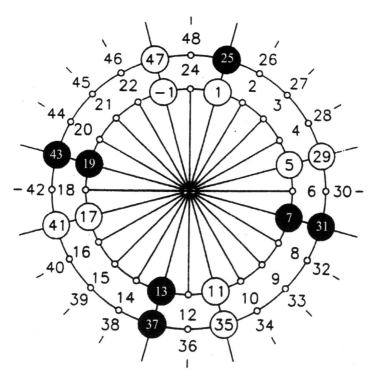

Figure 13. Plichta's first two rings of numbers, each of 24, with the prime numbers ringed. Seven of these, which are shaded, are also Bond and Lea's formative numbers.

with the exception of the number 25, they occur as alternate pairs in the series of prime numbers. Regarding the number 25, Plichta states "(In the inner ring) the number 24 is also found at point zero; 25 must therefore be located at a superimposed level above the 1; 26 above the 2 etc". The prime number 29 is above the prime number 5. Plichta's Figure 4 shows seven concentric rings, each of 24, ending at 168, with all the prime numbers combining to form a Templar cross. If, as he suggests for the two rings; these seven are seen as placed vertically, one above the other, then they can be seen to form a series of successively higher dimensions; the seven intervals in the musical octave and the rungs of Jacob's ladder.

Bond and Lea state "Mystically; Six is the Formative principle of the Cosmos.... But the Parent, whose immanence in his work gives Life; is the One, and hence the Unity must be added to give the Numbers of Perfection"[4] and hence the seven superimposed rings.

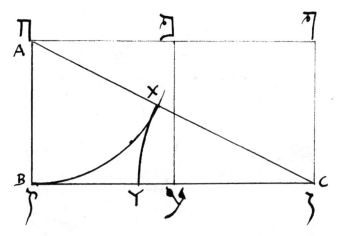

Figure 14. ABCD is a 2 × 1 rectangle, in which 2AB=CD. It represents two faces of two cubic modules from the AlephBaytic cube. A diagonal AC was drawn to give the right angle triangle ABC. The arc with centre A and radius AB was then drawn to cut AC at X. Then the arc with centre C and radius CX was drawn to find Y. The ratio BY:CY=1:1.618, the Golden Mean ratio. The ratio AB:AC=1:$\sqrt{5}$, 1:2.72, a close approximation to Euler's number 2.718.

Our authors point out that the highest Number of Perfection 43, raised by the power of Ten, is the number . . . of Number itself, 'arithmos' and Euler's number, 2.718, determines the distribution of prime numbers, as it does the rate of radio-active disintegration, the rate of decline in barometric pressure with height and all physical processes, which obey laws based on the natural log, Euler's number being based on the natural log to the base e, revealing Number as fundamental to the whole cosmos. In determining the distribution of the prime numbers in the descending series of creative energies, Euler's number provides a specific link with the whole of life and the underlying role of number in all physical manifestation. Euler's number, 2.718 (or its approximation 2.72), is also $\sqrt{5}$, expressed as the ratio 1:2.72. In Figure 1, the Aleph-Baytic cube, this ratio occurs, for example, as the ratio of the distance Zayn to Hhayt (7:8) in relation to that from Aleph to Hhayt (1:8), where Zayn to Hhayt is equal to 1. Aleph to Hhayt then equals 1 × $\sqrt{5}$, 2.72. Figure 14 shows such a rectangle ABCD, with a diagonal AD and two arcs intersecting at X to give Y, when the ratio DY:BY=1:1.618, the Golden Mean ratio. This ratio is present in the proportions of all living organisms, both plants and animals and in sacred architecture.[5]

Elohim, the Gods, written in Hebrew, is Aleph Lammed Hay Yod Mem (= 40, not Final Mem) has the gematria $86 = 2 \times 43$, the highest Number of Perfection. If we regard the 'Gods' as higher creative energies descending into the physical, it is only at the latter stage that polarisation into two (male and female, positive and negative etc.) takes place. This polarisation is implied by the $2 \times 43 = 86$ in the gematria of Elohim.

5

THE MYSTERY

In a discussion of the Greek 'to mysterion' (the Mystery), Bond and Lea show a series based on the gematria of 'phonē Kyriou' (The Voice of the Lord).[1] Table 2 lists another series of Greek terms that are in multiples of 100.

In this series of terms from the Greek text of the Book of Revelation, all multiples of 100, the key to an understanding of its meaning is in o geranos, the crane. Written without the article, as 'geranos', its gematria is 429, hence suggesting a link with arithmos, 'number', confirming that there is some deep significance in this series of numbers.

Robert Graves quotes Plutarch, who states that Theseus "introduced a Crane Dance into Delos (and) it was performed around a horned altar".[2] As we know, there was a major oracle centre and omphalos at Delos and it seems likely that the 'Horned altar' refers to the latter. Graves quotes Polwart's *Flyting with Montgomery* (1605):

> The crane must aye
> Take nine steps ere she flie.

Well, here in the series based on 100, we have eight of them. The next stage is to find the ninth step and the solution lies in the gematria of Apsinthion, which is 900. Multiplying this by $\sqrt{3}$ gives $900 \times 1.72 = 1548$, and this is the gematria of to mysterion, the mystery, which is also "the number of the incommensurable (unmeasureable) Line, the gramme asymmetros ... which is the parent of Rational Form and Whole Things – the Manifestations of the Aeons", as Bond and Lea put it.[3] But the ninth step in the Crane Dance involves the gramme asymmetros, the unmeasureable, expressed here as $\sqrt{3}$. Thus the ninth step involves taking off into the nonphysical realms and it is in achieving this raising of the level of consciousness above the mundane that the solution to the mystery is found.

Table 2.

Greek	English	
Apsinthion	Wormwood	$900 = 1548/\sqrt{3}$
Choinix	Measure	800
Phoinix	Phoenix	700
Kosmos	Cosmos	600
Iaspis	Jasper	501
Thronos	Throne	499
O geranos	Ther crane	499
Krios	Ram	400
Ars	Lamb	301
Ammon	Sand	201

However, just as with Jacob's angels (energies) going up and down the ladder, so there is a two-way flow in this series. The clue to this lies in the word apsynthion (wormwood): "...and there fell from heaven a great star...and the name of the star is called wormwood".[4] Here the "great star" suggests an energy source in a higher dimension, outside our three-dimensional world and in "falling" this energy is having its frequencies reduced to the range perceptible to our physical senses. The fact that the text goes on to describe the effects of this energy as harmful is not relevant. We are only concerned with the fact that its downward flow indicates energy flowing through the system in both directions.

Bond and Lea's series based on multiples of the gematria of 'phonē Kyriou', the Voice of the Lord,[5] gives at its 'sixth sounding', the number 14142.0. By moving the decimal point four places to the left this gives 1.4142, or $\sqrt{2}$, and leads to $\sqrt{3} \times 900$, which equals 1548, the gematria of 'to mysterion' (the Mystery). Bond and Lea say of their series it may "perhaps more fitly, be expressed as commencing with Unity". If we take this Unity to be the length of one side of the eight cubic modules in the AlephBaytic cube, then, as we saw, the length of the diagonals on the face of each module is equal to $1 \times \sqrt{2}$, while the ninth step of the Crane Dance is completed with $\sqrt{3}$, suggesting the internal diagonal of the cube. Putting Unity together with the two series we have a demonstration of the creation of the three-dimensional universe as exemplified by the cube of 27 Hebrew letters. The mystery lies in the means by which the Voice of God, the creative energy, becomes expressed in the sacred dance, which, in turn, brings the atoms of different elements together in crystalline form to make up the substance of our physical world.

Bond and Lea state that "The First Mystery is the Mystery of the Alpha — the Last...Mystery is the Mystery of the Omega.... But when the Pistis Sophia tells us that the First Mystery is also the (last), a riddle offers itself for solution, and this riddle can only be solved by reference to the geometry of the Alpha and the Omega".[6] What follows will point to a solution elsewhere and of a different kind.

Stan Tenen divides the first verse of the Book of Genesis into seven parts: In the beginning God created heaven and earth.[7] However, the reader will notice that this English translation has only six parts. In the Hebrew text there is a seventh, central, part, the fourth group of letters, which Tenen states cannot be translated: in the seven "days" of creation it is the Sabbath, the day of rest, i.e. when nothing is happening in the three-dimensional world. In Bond and Lea's series it is expressed by Unity and Unity multiplied by its square root (1.4142). It is the Still Point, the Source, from which all form originates.

In the Hebrew text, this untranslatable part consists of the letters Aleph and Tav, the first and last letters in the old Hebrew AlephBayt, hinting at what the Pistis Sophia calls the first mystery and the last mystery, what we have in the first chapter of Revelation as "I am Alpha and Omega, the first and the last". "The 24 Mysteria correspond to the 24 letters of the Greek Alphabet". With my first cyclical presentation of the numbers I had to account for how the number 24 can occur in the same place as the number 0".[8] The Pistis Sophia answers Plichta's problem with the statement that "the First Mystery is also the 24th mystery"[9] that region which lies outside the three dimensions indicated by the ring of 24, the Sabbath, when there was a pause in the creative process.

"And I turned to see the voice that spake with me. And having turned I saw seven golden candlesticks. And in the midst of the candlesticks one like unto a son of man...and his eyes were as a flame of fire".[10] Here the viewer is not turning, but is changing his position in relation to what he is viewing, so that what appeared to be a hexagon, seen in two dimensions, is actually a cube, as shown in Figure 1. In Figure 15 the Metacube is shown turned and with each of its constituent cubes drawn in relation to the Menorah, the candlestick with its central light and six branch lights. The central candle being the one "like unto a son of man" with eyes "as a flame of fire" this point being the centre of the AlephBaytic cube, the location of the letter Nun, meaning 'fish', hence Jesus's association with the fish vesica. This is surely not A son of man;

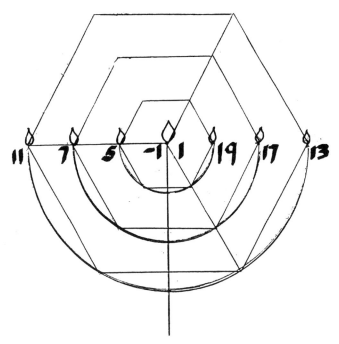

Figure 15. The central light and the lights on each of the six branches of the Menorah, each with its corresponding prime number from Plichta's first ring of 1 to 24. This is achieved by inverting Plichta's ring of 24, so that 11, 12 and 13 are at the top and dividing and folding down the two halves of the ring into a straight line.

but THE Son of Man, the embodiment of the Christ. The gematria of "like unto a son of man" is 1556, while "three darts"[11] in the Hebrew text also has the gematria 1556, while that of "resurrection of the body" in the Greek is 1554 (37 × 42), putting the Christ figure into the Osirian tradition of death and resurrection. Furthermore, "his eyes" in Greek has the gematria 841 and 840 (35 × 24) – the gematria of 'siderētēs', 'of iron', the lodestone from a meterorite, hence of siderial origin, from the stars. This suggests the seven stars which Bond and Lea relate to the Cube of Light,[12] and these 'stars' are the seven candles of the Menorah, as Revelation verse 12 suggests.

Figure 16 shows the central light and the lights on each of the six branches, each corresponding to one of the six prime numbers in Plichta's first ring of 1 to 24. To achieve this arrangement the ring is inverted, so that 12 is now at the top and it is divided here, with each part folded down, so that the numbers now form a straight line, with 1 at the centre. This now corresponds to Bond and Lea's series of seven, Unity

37

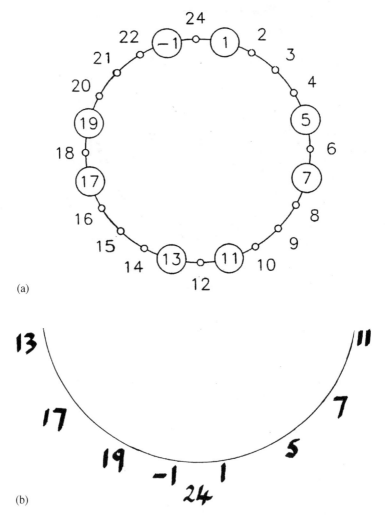

Figure 16. (a) Ring of first 24 numbers. (b) The ring inverted, divided at 12 and folded down with the first seven prime numbers shown.

and the six soundings of the Voice of God,[13] but with 1 (unity) now at the centre. In Plichta's first ring the number 24 is also in this central position, in accordance with the statement in the Pistis Sophia that "the First Mystery is also the 24th Mystery".

Turning now to the first verse of Genesis, Figure 17 shows each of Tenen's seven divisions with its corresponding candle in the Menorah, with Aleph Tav, the First and the Last at the central light. This confirms

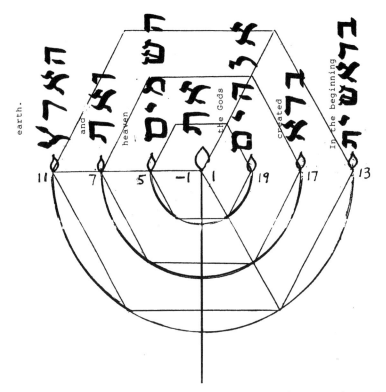

Figure 17. The menorah, the three cubes and the Hebrew text of Genesis, chapter 1, verse 1. The whole verse unfolds from the central, untranslated, group of Aleph Tav. These two letters correspond to −1 and 1, the hologram from which the plant develops.

that the statement "I am the Alpha and the Omega" (Revelation 1:8) refers to "in the midst of the candlesticks one like unto a son of man".[14]

Now we come to a most profound revelation concerning the Menorah: "And thou shalt make a candlestick of pure gold...and there shall be six branches going out of the sides thereof...three cups like almond blossoms in one branch, a bud and a flower and three cups like almond blossoms in the other branch, a bud and a flower".[15] The writers could hardly have made it clearer: we are dealing with a living system, the Tree of Life. Figure 18 shows a section through a flower of the rose family, with the parts of the flower numbered in accordance with the pairs of prime numbers in Plichta's first ring. At the centre is the embryo, with the seeds, corresponding to −1 and +1, that is containing the combination of male and female, the two poles inherent in all physical form. In the Hebrew text 'golden candlestick' has the gematria of 704, which is a key number in Bond and Lea's Cabala of

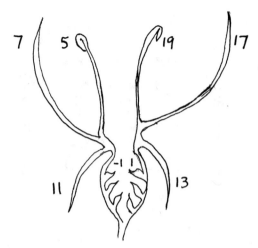

Figure 18. Vertical section through flower of rose family. The pairs of prime numbers are shown, as in Figures 15–17, with each pair equated with a part of the flower. 5 and 19 correspond to the stamens 7 and 17 correspond to the petals. 11 and 13 correspond to the sepals 1 and −1 correspond to the ovaries. The central light and the six branch lights are in the form of almond flowers in the Menorah and the almond is a member of the rose family.

the Fish.[16] In their diagram of the geometry associated with the Cabala (p. 54), the short axis of the vesica ABEF has a length of 704 and this is the gematria of the Greek 'ē katabolē ē parthēnia', the Virgin Conception and also of 'ē katabolē alētheias', the Conception of Truth, and 'ē ourania alētheia', the Higher Truth itself. This suggests that there is an immense complex of the deepest symbolic meaning surrounding the whole concept of the 'Menorah' expressed in the geometry (the Metacube), number (the prime numbers in the first ring of 24), the six + one lights of the Menorah and the six Voices of God + Unity in Bond and Lea's series; all expressed in the first verse of the Old Testament, the Uni.verse. In this verse we have the secret of the manifestation of the whole Universe. In his description of the 'seven golden candlesticks', the Writer of Revelation surely is aware of the symbolism as revealed here and is referring back to Genesis 1:1 and its relationship to the Menorah etc. so that, in a sense, Revelation is a recapitulation of the account of the creation of the Cosmos in Genesis 1:1.

In discussing the 'intrinsic meaning' of numbers derived from their essential nature, Bond and Lea remark on the "successive operation of the generative Power of the number Three".[17] This occurs, for example, in the three robes of Christ in the Pistis Sophia, in the three rays manifested in the Cube of Light and in the three groups of nine letters into which the Hebrew AlephBayt is divided and which appear in the three parallel planes of the AlephBaytic cube (see Figure 1). Another reference to the significance of the number three occurs in the first and last chapters of the Book of Revelation,[18] "I am the Alpha and the Omega . . . which is and which was and which is to come". In the Greek text 'kai o en' is translated as "and which was" and has the gematria 229. This is also the gematria of 'o anēr', the man, which suggests a link with "and in the midst of the candlesticks one like unto a son of Man",[19] which we know suggests the Christ. Bond and Lea show the hexagon with its central light[20] and the revelation of the cube of light when the hexagon is turned (see Figure 1). In turning the AlephBaytic cube the positions of three letters are revealed, Aleph, Nun and Final Tsadde, two opposite corners and the central point of the cube. Figure 19 shows that this central point is in the position of the central light of the Menorah, the location of "one like unto a son of man". The writer has already identified the two opposite corners, Aleph and Final Tsadde

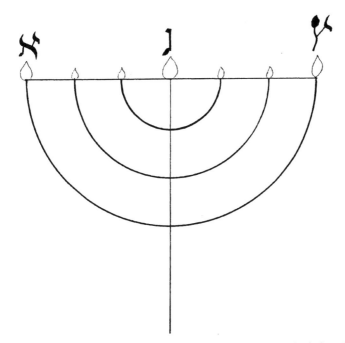

Figure 19. The Menorah and the AlephBaytic cube. Here we have the lights of the Menorah arranged along an internal diagonal of the cube of letters, between Aleph and Final Tsadde, with the central light at the central point of the cube, the position of the letter Nun: "That which is, that which was and that which is to come".

(Alpha and Omega) and now we have the Christ figure at the centre, "that which is and which was and which is to come". But these three points also express the internal diagonal of the cube, whose length in relation to a side of the cube is $1 : \sqrt{3}$, which, like "the relation of the Square root to Unity"[21] is aeonial.

Of these three points, the central one is also the terminal one of the Tree of Life (the Menorah) and this is the position of the letter Nun in the AlephBaytic cubes "And Moses called Hoshea the son of Nun Joshua [Latin form Jesus]", so that Jesus is the son of Nun. This confirms that the "one like unto a son of man" in chapter 1 of Revelation is Jesus. Furthermore, Jesus is descended through Joseph, from David, who was the son of Jesse, hence he is a "rod out of the stem of Jesse",[22] which, as we already know is in the Osiris/Salmon tree god tradition and this phrase from Isaiah clearly confirms the link with the tree/cross. So we have the Tree of Life/tree deity at the centre of the creative system through which the letters of the text bring the creative energies into physical form.

The word 'mystery' appears frequently in the English translations of the New Testament published in 1611 and 1884, as a translation of the Greek mysterion. However it is absent from both these versions of the Old Testament. Instead they give the word 'secret', as, for example, "the secret counsel of God",[23] which might alternatively be translated as "the mysterious counsel of God". The Hebrew word usually translated as 'secret' is Bayt Sammech Vav Dallet, whose gematria is 72 ($= 3 \times 24$) "And (Moses) . . . gathered seventy men of the elders of the people and set them round about the tent. And the Lord came down in the cloud, and spake unto (Moses), and took of the spirit that was upon him, and put it upon the seventy elders. . . . But there remained two men (Eldad and Medad): And the spirit rested upon them . . . but they had not gone out to the tent . . .".[24]

Here we have the gematria of 'secret', 72, suggesting a link with the seventy-two elders (including Eldad and Medad) and the gematria of 'tent' (Aleph Hay Lammed) is $36 = 72/2$ and being "set round about the tent", 36 also suggests the 360 degrees of a circle. Then we have "the Lord spake", suggesting the mysterion, expressed as the seven Voices of the Lord[25] and the seventy elders confirm this link (7×10). The cloud suggests an eletron cloud, i.e. energy, which is expressed as the 'Voice of the Lord'.

The Hebrew 'elders' is Zain Qof Nun Yod, whose gematria is 167 and $168 = 7 \times 24$, the central point and inner ring of Bond and Lea's Metakubon.[26] The gematria of Eldad and Medad, $39 + 58 = 97$ and

$96 = 4 \times 24$, another clear indication that we are dealing with the Metacube. The gematria of 'tent' in Hebrew (Aleph Hay Lammed) is $36 = 72/2$ and $36 \times 24 = 864$, the gematria of the phrase 'Kyrios demei', the Lord builds (his Tabernacle) and 'tent' is an alternative term for tabernacle, 36 being the total number of points in the Metakubon. This complex of gematria which are multiples of 24 suggests that this passage from the Book Numbers is a description of the setting up of a creative energy system to form the focal point, sustaining and promoting the well-being of the people of Israel. During the Exodus this had to be set up after each stage of the journey. All this gives a detailed description of the Mystery underlying the physical world.

Another English word, which might refer to something mysterious, is the adjective 'hidden', together with the verb 'to hide'. In Leviticus 5:2 the 1611 translation has "hidden from thee", in the sense of 'concealed'. and in Deuteronomy 30:11 it has "this commandment...is not hidden from thee...", both as translations of the Hebrew Hay Vav Aleph, whose gematria is 12, which fits, being equal to $24/2$, with the complex of multiples of 24 above, associated with the translation 'secret'. Then we have translations of the second person of the verb to hide, "thou hide" (in 1 Samuel 3:17) and "thee hide" (2 Samuel 14:8), as translations of the Hebrew Tav Kaf Hhayt Dallet, whose gematria is 432, which is equal to 18×24, where 18 is the number of points in Bond and Lea's outer ring in the Metacubon (p. 74) and is the gematria of 'tent' in the Hebrew text of Numbers 11:24. 432 is also the gematria of the Greek 'katabolē' (conception), which literally means 'thrown down' and of course the creative energies are literally being thrown down into the three-dimensional world.

As we know, each alternate prime number in Plichta's first and second rings is also one of Bond and Lea's Numbers of Perfection[27] (see Figure 14). Also, Plichta's three inner rings are completed by the number 72, and 71 is a prime number. The 70 'elders' together with Eldad and Medad can be regarded as a means of indicating an array of three rings and at the same time drawing attention to the prime number 71 and to the importance of prime numbers in general in the context of this array. The first number in Plichta's fifth ring is also the prime number 97, which is also the gematria of 'Eldad' and 'Medad', 39 and 58. Then we come to Plichta's seventh ring, in which the penultimate number is the prime 167 and this is the gematria of the Hebrew Zain Q of Nun Yod ('elders'). Again, as with $70 + 2$, not only does the gematria correspond with a prime number, but it points to an array based on 24 in each ring.

6

THE MYSTERY OF THE PISTIS SOPHIA AND THE NEW TESTAMENT

So far we have looked at the Mystery mainly from the point of view of the Hebrew text. Now, in considering Bond and Lea's *The First Mystery*,[1] we need to look for any correspondences between the evidence based on the gematria of the Hebrew text and the Greek text of the Pistis Sophia and the New Testament.

The Pistis Sophia refers to the second Endyma (the second of the three robes of Christ). This is one of the three robes, which refer to the three rays that form the basis of the Cube of Light.[2] The Pistis Sophia refers to this second robe as "the first precept [maxim]...the fifth charagmon, and mystery of the elders which is incapable of expression, which is the great light". In this passage the key to an understanding is the Greek 'charagmon', which means literally 'an engraven or emprinted mark'. However, in Bond and Lea's series of Voices of the Lord,[3] the fifth 'Voice' gives the number 1178.5, 1178 being the gematria of 'Mysterion', confirming that, as with the Hebrew text, we are indeed dealing with the Mystery and we now know, as indicated by that text, that the nature of this Mystery concerns the descent of higher creative energies into the three-dimensional world.

The next clue in this passage from the Pistis Sophia is in the Greek word here written as 'presbeutēs', meaning 'elder'. Bond and Lea point out that the usual form of this word lacks the second 'e' and that 'mysterion' also has an unusual spelling. Substituting the usual form, presbutes, we have the gematria 1295 (= 37 × 35), which is the gematria of the Hebrew Vav Sheen Phay Tav Yod Final Khaf ("thy lips[4]"), suggesting a link with the voice and therefore with Bond and Lea's series based on the Voice of the Lord. Furthermore, in the Greek text of Revelation 4:4, "twenty four elders" has the gematria 2884 and the gematria of the phrase 'to charagma tou kyriou' ('the sign, or mark, of the Lord'), has the gematria 2886 (= 37 × 78). We can now interpret this 'sign' as referring to the array of prime number patterns around the Tabernacle, or omphalos. All this demonstrates the remarkable degree of correspondence between the Hebrew and Greek texts revealed by the gematria and the way in which the two apparently unrelated texts, when combined in this way, give the true meaning.

Bond and Lea look at the gematria of *The First Mystery*, to 'A' Mysterion, 1549 and among other Greek terms with the same gematria is 'The Aeon of Jesus'. Looking at a possible Hebrew equivalent, we have the 'Aeon of David', which is Hay Aleph Hay Yod Aleph Lammed-Dallet Vav Dallet, whose gematria is 66 and 1549/66 = 23.47. If we call this 24 this gives a direct link to the gematria of Jesus in Greek, 888, which is equal to 37 × 24. David founded the bloodline of the Royal House of Judah and thereby initiated a stage in the process of cosmic creation, which was completed with the incarnation of the Christ as Jesus.

The place-name Gilgal also has gematria of 66: "And [Samuel] went from year to year in circuit, to Beth-el, and Gilgal, and Mizpah".[5] Jacob raised the stone he had used as a pillow, when he had his dream at Beth-el, as an omphalos and confirmed that it was a power centre by the statement "This is the House of God" which is the meaning of Beth-el. So it is likely that Gilgal and Mizpah are also the sites of omphaloi and that, in his yearly circuit, Samuel was checking that the energies were harmonious and flowing freely at each centre. The gematria of Beth-el, Gilgal and Mizpah add up to 719 and 720 = 30 × 24, the gematria of the Greek 'Topos', the Abode of Deity. Of course, as Jacob states, this is exactly what Beth-el is and, I suggest, the other two as well. 720 is also the gematria of Iereus, priest of the Temple of Truth, and clearly this is Samuel's role in making his circuit.

660 was the cabalistic number conventionally taken to represent the diameter of the earth, for it is a twelth of the actual diameter (7920) in miles. Therefore 66 in miles is 1/120th of the Earth's diameter, putting these three Benjamite towns into the context of a global system of omphaloi. "Two black doves flew away from Thebes in Egypt and one of them alighted at Dodōna, the other in Libya. The former, perched on an oak and speaking with a human voice, told them that there should be an oracle of Zeus". The other dove told the Libyans to form the oracle of Ammon, the Egyptian form of Zeus.[6]

The first thing to note about this account is that Thebes, Dodona and Siwa (where the oracle of Ammon was) are the equivalent of

Beth-el, Gilgal and Mizpah. Then the placenames themselves are revealing: the name Thebes comes from the Phonician 'Thibbun', a navel, and of course this is exactly, in a planetary sense, what were being established at Dodona and Siwa and there was an omphalos in the Temple of Ammon at Thebes, 'the geodetic centre of Egypt'. (Temple, loc. cit.). Furthermore, although Dodōna (the primary oracle centre in Greece) is in the north of the latter, "archaeology has confirmed remarkable parallels between Dodōna and Siwa. Furthermore; the cult of Amon in Siwa was associated with the deity Ddwn, which would seem to be the origin of the otherwise inexplicable name Dodōna".[7]

The 'black doves' in Herodotus's account are the equivalent of the dove and the raven which Noah sent out from the Ark (Genesis 3:8 and 9) and the raven "went forth to and fro" (verse 7); the 'flying shuttle'; weaving the new; post-diluvian energy fabric. Temple shows three examples of the triangulation system based on oracle centres round the eastern Mediterranean. One of these forms an equilateral triangle, corresponding to the triangle AEF in Figure 12 and Bond and Lea.[8] We saw in Figure 11 how this triangle relates to the whole cosmic scheme and we can now see how the latter underlies the laying out and physical manifestation of a new world; in this case after the Flood.

7

THE BREASTPLATE

Coming back to the Aeons, Bond and Lea state that "These endymata are the robes of Jesus; and are of the nature of the Aeons...".[1] 'Robe' in Hebrew is Mem Ayn Yod Lammed; whose gematria is 150 and that of the Greek endyma is 500, so that the three robes are equal to 1500 and this is equal to 150×10, a remarkable link between the Hebrew and the Greek texts.

But 1500 is the gematria of 'Endyma Kyriou', 'The Robe of the Lord', confirming the link with the Hebrew, and it is also the gematria of 'light' in Greek (phōs), so that; by putting on the royal robe of the priest-king, David, Jesus and all those who were "rods out of the stem of Jesse", became instruments of the manifestation of this Light as physical form.

"And when Saul enquired of the Lord; the Lord answered him not, neither by dreams; nor by Urim; nor by prophets".[2] In the English translations this clearly has nothing to do with light. However, the translation is defective, since 'Urim' is simply a transliteration of the Hebrew word Aleph Vav Raysh Yod Final Mem, meaning 'lights', so that the passage reads: "...neither by dreams, nor by lights, nor by prophets". The translators understandably couldn't make sense of this, being ignorant of gematria, so they fudged it and left 'Urim' untranslated.

Saul is facing the Philistines and "he was afraid and his heart trembled greatly" (verse 5), "the spirit of the Lord having departed from him".[3] In other words the robe of light of the priest-king had been withdrawn. This is confirmed by the failure of Saul's appeal to 'The Lord', by means of interpreting his dreams, by 'lights', or by prophecy. In the Hebrew text 'dreams' has the gematria 646 and $648 = 26 \times 24$, the gematria of 'House of Truth' (in Greek), while 'by prophets' in the Hebrew is 665 and $666 = 37 \times 18$, the gematria of Sammekh Vav Raysh Tav, which is the source of light; the fact that the text has the plural 'lights' is an indication that it is referring to the three robes which, in the plural endymata, has the gematria 1500, the gematria of phos (light).

So what were these 'lights' that Saul hoped would put him in touch with 'the Lord'? The answer lies in the "breastplate of judgement".[4] "And thou shalt put in the breastplate of judgement the Urim and the Thumim; and they shall be upon (the High Priest's) heart, when he goeth in (to the most holy place) before the Lord" (verse 30). This tells us that the 'lights' (the Urim) are part of the breastplate and that they are worn over the High Priest's heart when he goes into the Debir (the Most Holy Place, or place of the oracle). The breastplate is the work of "the cunning workman" (verse 15) and both words, 'cunning' and 'workman' in Hebrew have the root Hhayt Sheen, whose gematria is 308. This is the length of the temple at Luxor, measured in megalithic yards, suggesting that we are dealing with a temple of similar proportions. We also know that 'cunning workman' is a coded reference to one who understands and works with the relationship between the energies of the higher planes and those of the physical world. All this suggests that the High Priest, wearing the breastplate centred on his heart, was able to harmonise the higher energies flowing into the omphalos and then direct them out into the surrounding country. However, Saul's loss of this ability suggests that a high level of spiritual awareness was necessary to be able to do this.

In Hebrew 'breastplate' is Hhayt Sheen Final Nun, whose root Hhayt Sheen is the same as that of 'cunning' and 'workman', confirming the breastplate's cosmic, harmonic function. Its gematria with Final Nun included is 1008 and that of Oannes, the Sumerian half man, half fish, is 1009, whom we have seen is linked with the symbolism underlying the Baptism, i.e. the descent of higher energies into physical form. This is exactly what is happening as the High Priest works with the breastplate within the Debir, or oracular space. Furthermore, $1110 = 37 \times 30$, confirming that the process is taking place within the cosmic harmonic scheme whose base note is D, three octaves below middle C (see "time, times and half a time"[5]).

In the term 'breastplate of judgement', 'judgement' in Hebrew is Mem Sheen Pay Tayt, whose gematria is 429, that of the crane, 'geranos' in Greek, and this suggests the nine steps of the crane dance, the take-off into the Mystery of the higher planes of life. Working with the breastplate within the Debir, this is essentially what the High Priest does. Through his frailty Saul was not able to maintain the high level of spirituality to enable him to do this.

The Hebrew word for 'stone' used to refer to the jewels of the breastplate is Bayt Final Nun, 'ben' phonetically and we know that this is an Egyptian word. Astonishingly, the hieroglyph for this is:

an exact replica of the breastplate, as shown in Figure 20. This suggests that the whole system for working with higher energies described in Exodus 28 is essentially based on practices in temples in Ancient Egypt and this is confirmed by the gematria 308 in the roots of the Hebrew for 'cunning', 'workman' and 'breastplate' itself, 308 megalithic yards being the length of the Egyptian temple at Luxor. The gematria of Bayt Final Nun is 702 and $703 = 37 \times 19$, the gematria of Canaan in Greek, the land to which the Israelites made their Exodus from Egypt.

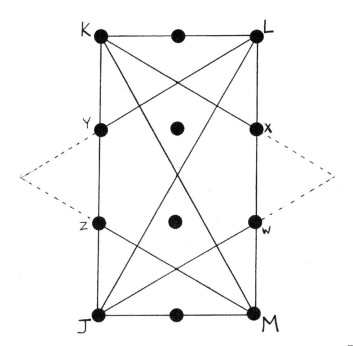

Figure 20. The breastplate. The twelve jewels of the breastplate are set in the $\sqrt{3}$ rectangle JKLM, where the width JM multiplied by 2 is equal to the diagonals JL and MK, the latter being given the base note and JM being one octave higher.

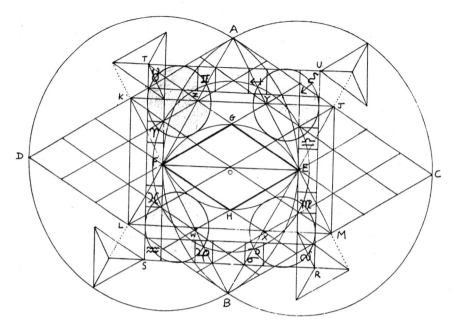

Figure 21. The oracular space. The rhombus EFGH represents a square viewed from an angle of 45 degrees to the vertical, the floor of the Debir, or Most Holy Place. The triangle AEF indicates the height of the floor at A.

Moses was a member of the Pharaonic royal house and there is a lot of evidence to suggest that the 'Israelites' whom he rescued were essentially low-cast Egyptians, the equivalent of the Harijans in India.

Figure 21 shows the breastplate, as described in Exodus 28:20. It is developed within the cosmic scheme, which is based on two intersecting circles. In the rectangle JKLM, the diagonals JL and KM are twice the length of JK, the width. In musical terms, if JK is an open pipe, such as an organ pipe, with a length of 2 feet, then it will give the note middle c, with a frequency of 264 Hz, and the diagonal will have a length of 4 feet, giving a frequency of 264/2, 132 Hz, the note c in the octave below. Equally, when JK = 2 feet, JX = 2 × 9/8 feet = 2 feet 3 inches, a ratio of 8:9, that of the major wholetone and an open pipe of this length will give the note b in the octave below.

Looking again at the equilateral triangle drawn within a square[6] (Figure 8), the triangle YKX in the breastplate is the same as AEO, where EO is half the length of one side of the containing square. In the same way, JKX is the same as AOF in Figure 8. As we saw, these triangles combine the musical proportions of the wholetone with the arithmetical ratio EO : AO, $1 : \sqrt{3}$. The same applies to the other wholetone triangles XJY, MLW and WZM, so that all the jewels round the perimeter are located according to arithmetical and musical proportions. The four jewels down the centre of the breastplate are located in the same way, but in triangles of half the size.

"And the stones shall be according to the names of the children of Israel, twelve . . . like the engravings of a signet".[7] The word 'names' in Hebrew is Sheen Mem Tav, whose gematria is 740 ($= 37 \times 20$), which Bond and Lea refer to as a "cosmic number". Greek words with this number include 'kyklos' (cycle) and 'ktisis' (creation), and Yod Kaf Yod Final Nun of the Hebrew temple symbolism,[8] where this Hebrew word Jakin refers to one of the two pillars on either side of the entrance to Solomon's temple. We already know that in Figure 12, the Cosmic Scheme and the triangle within the square, the rhombus ABCD is Solomon's magic carpet, the magic square of the Sun viewed from an angle of 45 degrees and this has sides of 6×6. The rhombus with long axis EF and centre 0 can be regarded as a scaled down version of the magic carpet/magic square of the Sun. If we now see it as the base of a cube, its 6×6 proportions correspond to the floor of the Debir, with its sides and roof raised above to form the $6 \times 6 \times 6$ cube of that oracular space. The diagonal of the floor is EF and this is also a side of the square EFGH and of the equilateral triangle AEF, within which the arithmetic, geometric and musical proportions are synthesised. The sides of the Debir are equal to the diagonal $EF/2 = 6/8$.

On the same scale $AO = 7/8$, as does JM. Taking the rectangle as the plan of the whole temple, with the two pillars, Jakin and Boaz, at J and M, this links the proportions of the temple, including the Debir, to the musical proportions, JM being the tonic or base note of the rectangle JKLM. The breastplate is therefore a small-scale version of the whole temple and, standing at the centre of the Debir, with the breastplate centred on his heart, the High Priest can resonate with and direct the creative energies within the system. Energy flowing into the Cosmic Scheme at C sets up a resonance between the pillars Jakin and Boaz, at J and M, which has the frequency of the base note of the whole system. Pillars at K and L, and at W, X, Y and Z, then resonate at their different frequencies within the octave indicated by the distances JM and JL/MK, where the latter are one octave below JM. The gematria of Jakin in Hebrew is 740 and we saw that in the Hebrew text of "time, times and half a time",[9] the Hebrew for 'time' has the root Ayn Dallet, whose gematria is 74. We saw that the two octave series based on this phrase from Daniel is D_1, D and d, where the middle note has the frequency 74 Hz, suggesting a link between the musical system based on Jakin and Boaz and this two octave series.

"And within the oracle was a space of twenty cubits in length, and twenty cubits in breadth, and twenty cubits in the the height thereof...".[10] Here 'the oracle' is Hay Dallet Bayt Yod Raysh, whose gematria is 221, which fits with the dimensions of $2 \times 2 \times 2$ cubits described. We have identified the Debir as the inner rhombus with long axis EFGH in Figure 21. Outside this is the 4×4 rhombus with long axis E'F' and then the 6×6 rhombus ABCD. This suggests, in terms of the underlying geometry, the Holy of Holies, the Inner Court and the Outer Court respectively. We already know that the AlephBaytic cube has proportions of $2 \times 2 \times 2$, that Bond and Lea's Metacube is $4 \times 4 \times 4$ and Debir has the gematria of 216, which equals $6 \times 6 \times 6$. Verse 20 (see above) states that there was 'a space' with dimensions of $20 \times 20 \times 20$ $(2 \times 2 \times 2)$ within the oracle, which fits with this picture of the oracle containing other spaces. Verse 36 states "(Solomon) built the inner court with three rows of hewn stone...", where the three rows may refer to the three concentric rhombuses. Here the word 'inner' in Hebrew is Aleph Tav-Hay Hhayt Tsadde Raysh, whose gematria is 704, the gematria of the Greek phrase "The True Conception", "the Conception of Truth" and "the Higher Truth itself". In their Cabala of the Fish Bond and Lea reveal this number 704 as the basis for a whole network of terms from the Greek text.[11] "We have set out this series (based on 704) in some detail... (and) it is clear that the symbol refers not only to the Christian Faith..., but, by this body of geometrical teaching, to its Founder as well, as the word of Truth proceeding from the Father and through the Spirit".[12] But EF in our Cosmic Scheme (Figure 10) corresponds to the radius of the two overlapping circles in Bond and Lea's geometry, to which they give the value 704, and this has enabled us to extend their Cabala far beyond the limits of Christianity, to one that is truly cosmic, by combining it with the Hebrew text of the Old Testament. "Jesus said; Destroy this temple, and in three days I will raise it up.... But he spake of the temple of his body"[13] (John 2:19). But the gematria of "this temple" in the Greek text of John's gospel is 591 and $592 = 37 \times 16$, which is also the gematria of the Greek 'agiotes' (holy), as in the Most Holy Place, or Debir. As Schwaller de Lubicz shows in *The Temple of Man*, the human body and the temple as a building are intimately connected in their proportions and Jesus was surely aware of this and was referring to both as essentially expressions of the same cosmic proportions. The figure of Christ in Glory in Christian art shows the figure of Jesus Christ within the vesica piscis, for example in ABEF in Figure 10, where the height of his body corresponds to AB and its width to EF, so that the proportions of his figure literally determine the proportions of the whole Cosmic Scheme and therefore of the Cosmic Temple, as we have discovered it.

In Revelation 1:12 and 13 we saw that the figure "in the midst of the candlesticks, like unto a son of man" is the Christ and that He stands at the centre of the AlephBaytic cube, the position of the Hebrew letter Nun, as revealed in the turned cube, shown in Figure 1. In the unturned cube, as it appears in the Cosmic Scheme (Figure 10) this central point and two of the corners of the cube are in line at 0, hence, paraphrasing Revelation 1:8, "I am Aleph and Final Tsadde; that which is; and which was, and which is to come". In Cephas,[14] in their diagram of the cube of nine, only one of the 243 squared stones making up "the Perfect Stone upon which Christ built His Church . . . shows three facets (and) this represents the Chief of the Seven corner stones and the triple Divine Potency".[15] Clearly the 'Triple Potency' refers to the centre and two corners in line at O in the Cosmic Scheme. In Revelation 1:14 there is a reference to the head of the Christ figure and in the Greek text 'head' is 'kephale'. Bond and Lea refer to the expression 'kephale gonias', "an epithet of Christ" in Matthew 21:42, "the Head of the Corner", whose gematria is 1628, which is equal to 37×44. Figure 38 shows the cube reversed, so that Aleph is at the front corner, the starting point of the AlephBayt, the Foundation Stone of the system. Aleph is written as Aleph Lammed Pay, whose gematria is 111 ($= 37 \times 3$), where the three ones suggest Bond and Lea's Triple Potency. This corresponds to Bond and Lea's cube showing three facets.

In Hebrew 'head' is Raysh Aleph Sheen, whose gematria is 501 and in Revelation 4:4 we have "And round about the throne were four and twenty thrones and upon the thrones I saw four and twenty elders sitting . . .". In the Greek text 'thronos' (throne) has gematria 501, the same as that of the Hebrew 'head', confirming that 0 in the Cosmic Scheme and the position of Aleph in the AlephBaytic cube are the same. The "four and twenty elders" put the whole Temple creative system into the mathematical context of Plichta's rings of 24 and Bond and Lea's Numbers of Perfection.[16]

In their reference to the "Head of the Corner" (p. 68) Bond and Lea quote from Matthew 21:42, but this is itself a quotation from Psalms 118:22. "The stone which the builders rejected" in the Hebrew has the gematria 1501 and, as we know, the gematria of the Greek 'phos' is 1500. At the centre of the Menorah (the six-branched candlestick) stands "one clothed like unto a son of man"[17] and this is also the position of the letter Nun in the AlephBaytic cube and these lie in line with the front corner of the cube, at 0 in the Cosmic Scheme. 'Endyma [500] is one of the many mystical words used by St. Paul. The Pistis Sophia has three of these robes of light and $3 \times 500 = 1500$.[18] All this confirms that the Christ-figure in Revelation 1:13 and the central candle of the Menorah are located at 0 in the Cosmic Scheme and that it is this Light that is the Source of the whole Creation. Standing at the centre of the system, in the position of Nun in the AlephBaytic cube, the Priest of the Order of Melchizadek uses the twelve stones of the breastplate to modulate the frequencies of the Light from the point source at C, after it has been polarised at J and M, the pillars Jakin and Boaz. The Priest then speaks the Hebrew words containing the appropriate letters, which in turn sets up harmonic resonance with the corresponding locations of those letters within the AlephBaytic cube and "the Oracle speaks", sending out enlivening energies into the surrounding land.

8

THE SALMON

"And the word of the Lord came to Solomon, saying: concerning this house which thou art building, if thou wilt walk in my statutes and execute my judgements, and keep all my commandments...then will I establish my word with thee...and I will dwell among the children of Israel...".[1]

"The word of the Lord" suggests 'phonē Kyriou' (the Voice of the Lord, whose gematria is 2358, one of Bond and Lea's seven mysteries.[2] As we know 'to mysterion' concerns the means by which the creative energies are translated into physical form and the temple that the Salmon (Solomon) is 'building'. So 'the Lord' is imparting the secrets of the mysteries associated with sacred buildings and the way they work. ("And God gave Solomon wisdom and understanding.")[3]

Salmon (Solomon) in Hebrew is Sheen Lammed Mem Hay, whose gematria is 375. Does this offer us any clues as to the role of the Salmon? As we know, the name 'Salmon' is a title, in the same sense as 'Pharaoh' in the Egyptian tradition. In the latter Amon-Ra was the Godhead, the Creative Source and patron of the Pharaohs. In the Cosmic Scheme he stands at the centre, in the position of Nun in the cube of Hebrew letters, the "One like unto a Son of Man" in Revelation 1:13. Amon-Ra in Greek has the gematria of 592 ($= 37 \times 16$) and this is also the gematria of Theotes, the Godhead, and Exegetes, the Interpreter, in the sense that he stands between heaven and earth, transposing the higher energies into physical form as they flow through the Cosmic Scheme, acting through the Pharaoh/Salmon.

The two words Salmon Debir in Hebrew have the gematria $375 + 216$, which equals 591, confirming the role of the Salmon as 'Interpreter' at the centre of the Oracle, or Debir, at the centre of the cube of letters. All this places the Hebrew sacred creative system firmly within the Egyptian tradition. Referring again to Revelation 1:13, "Son of Man"

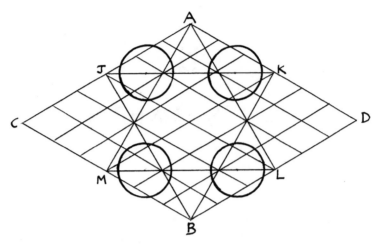

Figure 22. The Salmon's tools. Solomon's magic carpet, the 6 × 6 rhombus ABCD and the four jewels of his magic ring, both bound together by his seal, AKLBMJ.

can be written as Sun o' Man, or Sol o' Man, the Sun symbolising the source of all physical life.

Figure 22 shows the Salmon's 'tools'. These consist of his magic carpet, the 6 × 6 rhombus ABCD, which forms the outer court of the temple. Turned through 45 degrees, so as to view it from a vertical angle, it forms the magic square of the Sun, which fits with the Solomon's role as the 'Sun o' Man', the Solar Being. The total of all the 36 numbers in this magic square adds up to 666, which is equal to 37 × 18 "... originally appertaining to the Solar Divinity ... in the Hebrew ... Sheen Mem Sheen-Yod Hay Vav Hay, Shemesh-Yaweh, the Sun of Yaweh".[4] This confirms the Salmon's role as the Sun o' Man. "And (the Ark) came into the field of Joshua the Beth-Shemite and stood there, where there was a great stone".[5] Here the 'great stone' is clearly an omphalos associated with the Beth-Shemite solar energies. The whole of this account in 1 Samuel 6:8–14 is intended to show the immense power drawing the Ark towards the omphalos. 'Shemesh' means literally 'named mesh' or 'net', and this is exactly what it is: the 6 × 6 net, or lattice named after the Sun. On a planetary scale it consists of the energy lines forming a network between all the 'world navels', or omphaloi.

The diagram showing the Salmon's tools demonstrates the way in which the six-pointed star ties the magic carpet, ABCD, to the four jewels of the magic ring. No wonder this double triangle is referred to as 'Solomon's seal', since it seals the carpet and ring into one geometric whole; with its points J, K, L and M establishing the musical proportions, in which JM is the base note and the ratio JM:JL etc. give the octave and so on. Stirling[6] shows a "sigil from Kircher's Arithmologia", in which Kircher has drawn a 5×5 square within the hexagram. The square suggests the 5×5 magic square of Mars, rather than the 6×6 square of the Sun and therefore not suggesting any link with the Salmon. The letters make a Latin epigram, "but it is apparently untranslatable". However, the first word read from right to left is 'rotas', 'wheels'. We know that the four jewels in the magic ring are in the shape of a whale, an eagle, a lion and a serpent. These correspond to Ezekiel's four 'creatures':[7] "I beheld the living creatures, behold one wheel upon the earth; beside the living creatures for each of the four faces thereof" (verse 15), i.e. one wheel for each jewel. The 'wheels' are the four circular settings of the jewels (see Figure 6). Ezekiel goes on "As for their rings, they were high and dreadful; and they four had their rings full of eyes round about" (verse 18). I believe that these rings are the orbital paths of electrons and that the 'eyes' are the electrons themselves. Ezekiel writes that the appearance of the living creatures "was like burning coals of fire ... as the appearance of a flash of lightning" (verses 13 and 14), suggesting the nuclear energy latent within the atom. Recalling that each 'jewel' corresponds to one of the four fundamental forces and that, of these, one represents strong nuclear force that which holds the nucleus of the atom together, and the other relates to weak nuclear force, which concerns the nuclear activity of stars, it seems at least likely that whoever wrote this passage of Ezekiel knew about subatomic particles and the structure of atoms. Perhaps we need to consider the possibility that modern 'discoveries' about atomic structure etc. may be only rediscoveries of what was known long ago, that those in the Salmonic/Pharaohic tradition not only knew the theoretical aspects of quantum physics, but how to work with the enormous forces involved, in order to promote the well-being of the Earth and all its creatures.

Ezekiel states: "for the spirit of the living creature was in the wheels",[8] making it clear that we are dealing with the basis of life. "Spirit whirleth about continually and returneth again according to his circuits",[9] says Solomon. Verse 5 has "The sun also ariseth, and the sun goeth down", as Blavatsky says the original text refers "both to the spirit and to the sun". The gematria of Sheen Lammed Mem Hay (Solomon) is 375 and $4 \times 375 = 1500$, the gematria of the Greek 'phōs' (light), so that he is indeed the Sun, embodied in the four jewels of the magic ring, the one "like unto a son/sun of man" in Revelation 1:13. In fact as Sun o' Man, he embodies the whole creative system pictured in the Cosmic Scheme.

The second word in Kircher's sigil is 'opera', 'a work' and the whole three-dimensional Universe can be regarded as the work of the Salmonic/ Pharaohic Being, working within the Cosmic Scheme. He is, in the Hebrew canon, "appertaining to the Solar Divinity, ... Shemesh Yaweh – the Sun of Yaweh"[10] (Bond and Lea, p. 66), the Solomon; or Sun o' Man.

Coming back to Kircher's sigil, Stirling (p. 272) states that rotas (wheels) written in Greek letters, "has the numerical value of 671, the number of Thora, the Hebrew Bride and the Greek o Kosmos = 670", while the Hebrew Yod Hay Vav Hay Aleph Lammed Hay Yod Final Mem, 'the Sons/Suns of Yaweh' has the number $672 = 28 \times 24$, suggesting Mother and Sons in the Cosmic Creative process. The middle letter (of the sigil) is N, Nun in Hebrew and this is the central letter of the cube of Hebrew letters and the location of "one like unto a son of man".[11] This confirms that Kircher's sigil refers to the Salmon and the Cosmic Scheme.

Figure 23 shows the flow of energy through the Cosmic Scheme. The flow originates from a uni-polar source at C and becomes bi-polar at M and J, the pillars Jakin and Boaz. It flows on from M through E, Y, Z, F, L and D. The wave form is that of alternating electricity: the path rotates around the axis CD, so that it alternates between M, E, Y, Z, F and L and J, E, X, W, F

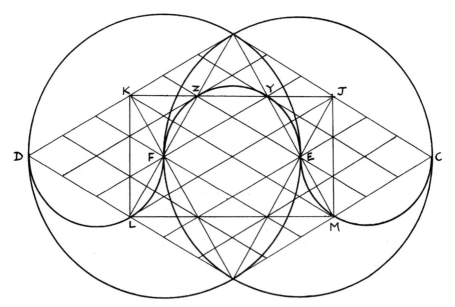

Figure 23. The energy flow through the Cosmic Scheme. The flow is from C, through M, E, Y, F and L to D, or the reverse, from D, through K, F etc. to C.

and K. Taking each of the circles with centres at E and F and radius EF, the path followed by the energy within each of these circles makes a Yin Yang pattern, suggesting a balance between the Solar and Lunar, masculine and feminine/positive and negative, which, of course, reflects the bi-polar nature of the energy imparted by Jakin and Boaz as it enters the three-dimensional world. The two pillars set up an electro-magnetic field within the Cosmic Scheme. The fusion of sperm and egg at the moment of conception involves the same development of a bi-polar state as the soul enters the physical world.

Bond and Lea look at the 'Greater Light', "the number of the First Precept of the Omnipotent", whose gematria in the Greek, 'phōs mega', is 1549. They have already established that 'phōs', whose gematria of 1500 relates to the three robes of Christ, where the gematria of endyma (robe) is 500 and $3 \times 500 = 1500$. "Regarding then the 1549 of this Mysterion ('phōs mega') as the arithmetical sign of this Power, let us now look at its parent number. Now as $\sqrt{3}:3::1549:2683$, 2683 is the parent Number, indicative of the Creator of Light."

We have already seen that the bi-polar basis of the three-dimensional world is expressed in the Yin Yang symbol traced by the energy pathway through the overlapping circles in the Cosmic Scheme. Yin corresponds to the Moon and Yang to the Sun, whose numbers are respectively 1080 and 666. "The sum [of these two numbers] of the symbolic number of Yang, positive and Yin, negative forces respectively", combine to give the number 1746, the parent Number, as Bond and Lea express it. "According to the ancient cosmogony, creation issues from the union of these two forces, and the primal unit of creation was known in allegory as 'kokkos sinapeos', a grain of mustard seed".[12] All three synoptic gospels describe it as "the least of all seeds from which sprang the tree of the universe". The gematria of 'kokkos sinapeos' (the mustard seed) is 1746, "the number of fusion, because it is the sum of 666 and 1080 and 1746 divided by $22/7$ $(\pi) = 555 = 37 \times 15$ and the Hebrew Mem Raish Aleph Hay-Aleph Sheen 'appearance of fire'[13] has the gematria 554, suggesting Ezekiel's vision".[14] John Michell gives a whole page of expressions which, in Greek, have gematria of 1746,[15] including 'the Divine Man', 'the Spirit of the Universe' and 'the Spiritual Universe and these are comparable with the examples Bond and Lea give of phrases with the gematria 2683 expressing the parent Number, "indicative of the Creator of Light". "These magnificent words, so grand, so simple and telling, all occurring on this individual number, bespeak some great principle to be looked for".[16] If we look at another example of such a 'telling' phrase, 'ē katabolē alētheias',[17] whose gematria is 704, here we find this number expressed in their diagram of the Cabala of the Fish, where it is EF, the radius of the two overlapping circles.

Figure 24 shows the stages in the development of the Cosmic Scheme, starting with a circle and its central point, the cabalistic sign

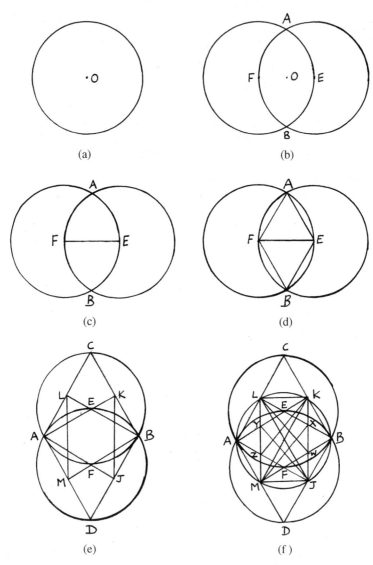

(a)

(b)

(c)

(d)

(e)

(f)

Figure 24. (a) A circle with centre O. (b) The fish vesica, opening of the mouth. (c) EF, the OM phalos, the instrument. (d) The rhombus ABEF composed of two equilateral triangles. (e) Solomon's seal: the six pointed star ALKBJM. (f) The $\sqrt{3}$ rectangle JKLM, where $2 \times JM = JL$. $JM:JZ=8:9$, the major wholetone. $JM:JY=2:3$, the musical fifth.

for the Sun. Stage (c) shows the first point at which a straight line, AB, appears. This corresponds to AB in Figure 23, showing the flow of energy through the Scheme. This line is the first stage in the manifestation of the physical world, corresponding to the erect penis in depictions of the ithy-phallic Pharaoh in Egyptian art. In the cabalistic Tree of Life, the whole tree grows from the Prima Sephira, shown as the resting state, with the potential for creation, the finite, bi-polar condition, contained within the circle of infinity. This fits with EF being equal to 704 in Bond and Lea's diagram, since the act of conception is an example of the emergence of Creative Energy from within the circle.

In Figure 23 showing the flow of energy through the Cosmic Scheme, we have the same underlying structure as in Bond and Lea's Cabala of the Fish, but here EF is equal to 277.5 ($=555/2$) As they point out, the ratio EF:AB is equal to $1:\sqrt{3}$, since ABEF is a vesica piscis and this proportion is a characteristic of its geometry. If we then multiply 277.5 by $\sqrt{3}$, we get 480 and $481 = 37 \times 13$, the gematria of the Greek 'ē genesis', the Beginning, and the vesica ABEF is indeed the beginning, the womb in which the creative energies flowing in from C are reduced in frequency to the point at which they become perceptible to our physical senses and become part of what we call 'reality'.

9

THE TEMPLE OF MAN

Bond and Lea develop a whole constellation of significant Greek phrases whose gematria correspond to the proportions of their diagram of the Cabala of the Fish,[1] most of which relate to $\sqrt{3}$. An attempt to apply the value of $\sqrt{3}$ to the similar diagram based on circles with a diameter of 555, rather than Bond and Lea's based on circles with radii of 704 produces one significant value as we have found above: $277.5 \times \sqrt{3} = 480$ and this is the height of the Great Pyramid expressed in feet. This points, not in the direction of expressions from the Greek text of the New Testament, but to Ancient Egypt and a cosmic view, which fits with the picture presented by our investigation of the Hebrew text of the Old Testament.

This is confirmed by the value for the distance CD in the Cosmic Scheme, which is 832.5, 831 being the gematria of the Greek 'pyramis', 'pyramid'. Figure 25 shows John Michell's "Pyramid formed by circles of circumference 1746 ft".[2] This shows the two intersecting circles from our Cosmic Scheme contained within the two intersecting arcs of a larger vesica piscis, with their centres at C and D. We already know that, when the vesica ABEF is formed within intersecting circles of 555 feet diameter, the distance AB is 480 feet and this is the height of the Great Pyramid, so A is the apex of the Pyramid. Michell draws a line GBH and links each end of this to the apex at A, forming a Great Pyramid triangle characterised by the base angles AGB and AHB of 51 degrees 51 minutes[3] to give the following measurements:

EF = 277.5 feet

CD = 277.5 yards (1 yard = 3 feet)

GH = 277.5 megalithic yards (1 MY = 2.72 feet, 0.829 m)

AB = 280 Royal Cubits (1 RC = 1.72 feet)

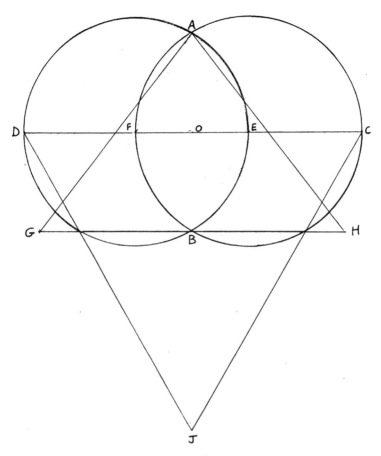

Figure 25. The Great Pyramid and circles of 555 diameter. CF and DE=555, EF=277.5, AB=480 feet (the height of the Great Pyramid).

"The completed figure provides a unique diagram of the five units of sacred measure and the way in which they are related to each other". Furthermore, they are related as the roots of numbers, in the same way in which the letters in the AlephBaytic cube are related to each other in the formation of significant words from the text within the cube. The total length of the base perimeter of the pyramid is equal to $4 \times 277.5\,\mathrm{MY} = 1110\,\mathrm{MY}$ and $1110 = 37 \times 30$, the gematria of the Greek 'o mikros kosmos', the microcosm and this is what the Pyramid is, since it embodies proportions expressed in sacred measure which are universal.

We have already looked at energy pathways into and through the Cosmic Scheme, for example in Figure 24, where the energy emanates from C and flows into the system through the two pillars Jakin and Boaz. In the case of the Great Pyramid system, the two circles of fusion, with their circumference of 1746, the gematria of 'kokkos sinapeos', the mustard seed, suggests a single intense energy entry point and the shape and colour of this seed "the seed of fire", suggests the Sun. The apex of the Pyramid, according to John Michell, has a tip "which is formed by a gold pyramid of 5 cubic inches" with a diamond or some other crystal at its tip, which is symbolised by the mustard seed. This tiny intense tip at the apex of the massive bulk of the Pyramid is the nearest we can get to the conception of infinity. In relation to the Cosmic Scheme, viewing the Pyramid from directly above, the jewel at the apex is at 0 and the four corners of the base correspond to the four jewels of the Salmon's magic ring, with the higher energies pouring into the apex and down through the enormous physical bulk of the Pyramid and out into the world through the corners. Piazzi Smith (Our Inheritance in the Great Pyramid, quoted by John Michell[4]) found "that the latitude of its site is 30 degrees north, exactly one third of the distance from the Equator to the Pole. The Pyramid is placed on the northern extremity of the range of hills commanding the entire plain of Lower Egypt" and is at the centre of an arc which follows the coast of the Nile Delta. The meridian line which runs due north south "and bisects the Pyramid's base; contains more land and less sea than any other". All this suggests that the energies flowing from the Pyramid's base were designed to be a major factor in maintaining the well-being of the Planet and her creatures.

"The Pyramid belongs above all to Mercury, or Hermes. . . . The pentacle of Mercury, of which the Great Pyramid is the traditional emblem, relates to the eight-sided square", the magic square of Mercury and this 8×8 square, making a total of 64, is a two-dimensional representation of the Metacube, with its 64 points. In Bond and Lea's scheme, where each point has a value of 24, $64 \times 24 = 1536$, the gematria of the Greek The True Geometry[5] and the Great Pyramid is the perfect example of this.

Esoteric tradition suggests that there is a mirror image below the Pyramid, which is yet to be discovered. Together they form a Great Pyramid octahedron. Figure 26 confirms the existence of this lower half, since the distance AB is equal to BK, 480 feet 6 inches, so that the distance AK is 961 feet and $962 = 37 \times 26$. The heavenly fire that Prometheus stole from the gods is 'to entechnon pyr', the artificer's fire, whose gematria is 2080 which "bears the same relationship to the power of Mercury as does the number 666 to solar energy, for, as 666

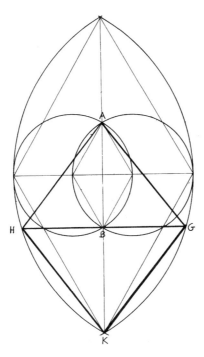

Figure 26. The Great Pyramid octahedron AGKH, where the hidden lower half KGH is a mirror image of the upper, visible half, AGH.

is the total sum of numbers in the magic square of the Sun, so 2080 is the sum of the numbers in the square of Mercury. . . . There is, therefore, every possibility that the Great Pyramid was constructed to create a fusion of two elements, celestial and terrestial".[6] Michell states that by convention the meaning of 2080 is the same as 1080, which, along with the solar number 666; makes up the interlocking circles of fusion with centres at E and F. So, since the upper part of the Pyramid, AGH in Figure 26 receives the solar energy, then the lower part, KGH, receives the terrestial energy and the Pyramid is an instrument for the fusion of these two and their radiation into the surrounding land. Since we have forgotten the existence of the lower half of the Pyramid, this creative process is no longer taking place and the results of this are plain to see.

Looking again at the dimensions of the Great Pyramid, one side of the base measures 444 Royal Cubits and $444 = 37 \times 12$, while the diagonal of the base is $444 \times \sqrt{2} = 628$, the gematria of Tiberias in Greek, the Roman name for the Sea of Galilee, where, described in John 21, Jesus gave a demonstration of the creative process. The lake acts as the

Table 3.

Plan	Body of Pharaoh
JM: position of statue of Pharoah and Queen in Outer Court	Queen's fingertips on back of Pharoah's leg
WZ	Pharoah's fist
C: door from Colonnade to Inner Court	Base of Pharaoh's spine
XY	Pharaoh's Belt
KL: inner row of columns	Pharaoh's armpits
Hypostyle hall	Lower edge of head-dress at front

amnion, in which the 'fishes', i.e. energy, are 'caught' in the net, i.e. crystallised into physical form. The Pyramid carries out the same process.

We know that the temple at Luxor has an overall length of 308 megalithic yards (MY) and in feet this is 832.5 (308×2.72) and the gematria of the Greek 'pyramis' is 831. Figure 27 shows the two inter-locking circles of fusion/with centres at E and F and a diameter of 555 feet. $555 \times 3/2 = 832.5$, so that, as the drawing shows, the overlapping circles exactly fit the length of the temple, with C at the outer side of the inner wall of the Covered Temple, and D at the outer side of the Outer Court, with AB determining the position of the wall between the colonade and the Inner Court in the temple plan and the base of the coccyx in the human body. With the rectangle JKLM and its musical proportions drawn, many significant points in the plan and human body are revealed to be based on musical proportions.

The reader may question the need for this detailed examination of the musical etc. proportions of the temple and body. In the drawings in Figures 27 and 28 based on R. A. Schwaller de Lubicz's *Le Temple de l'Homme*, he was setting out to demonstrate the similarity between the proportions of the temple and those of the human body and to show that the stages in the development of the body from birth to adulthood correspond to stages in the building of the temple.

Here we are concerned with the role of the High Priest in the functioning of the temple as a receiver, transformer and transmitter of creative energies. The High Priest's role in this process is dependent on the fact that the proportions of his body correspond to those of the temple, so that harmonious resonance can be established between him and the temple in which he is working. The High Priest stands within the Debir, or oracle and is bathed in the creative energies. By being consciously aware of these vibrations, he is able to modulate and

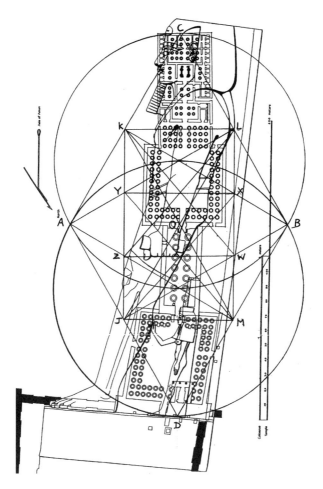

Figure 27. Pharaoh and Queen on temple plan. Musical proportions.

control them, thereby promoting the health and well being of the people, plants and animals living in the surrounding area.

"And these are the garments which they shall make; a breastplate, and an ephod, and a robe, and a coat of chequer work, a mitre, and a girdle: and they shall make holy garments for Aaron, thy brother, and his sons, that he may minister unto me in the priest's office. And they shall take the gold, and the blue and the purple, and the scarlet, and the fine linen".[7] In this passage 'garment' is Bayt, Gimmel Dallet, whose gematria is 9, while 'breastplate' is Hhayt Sheen Final Nun, whose gematria is 1008 and 1008/9 = 112 = 8 × 14. 'Chequer work' in the Hebrew is Tav Sheen Bayt Final Tsadde, whose gematria is 1602 and 1602/9 = 178,

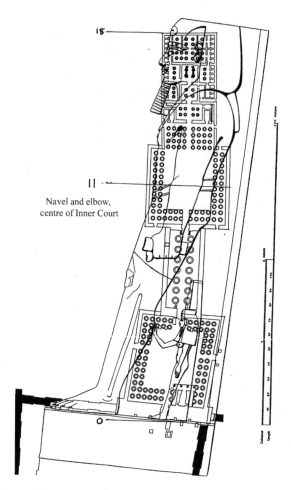

18

11

Navel and elbow,
centre of Inner Court

Figure 28. Division of Pharaoh and temple plan by 18.

while $178/112 = 1.55$, just over $1\frac{1}{2}:1$. The occurrence of 9 hints at the ennead of 3×9 letters in the AlephBaytic cube. Chequer work suggests magic squares and the gematria of 'mitre' in Hebrew is 660, hinting at the magic square of the Sun, a 6×6 square with a total of 666.

The reference to the four colours, gold, purple, blue and scarlet, as we know, refers to the four jewels in the Salmon's magic ring and to the four fundamental forces of modern physics, while the "fine twined linen" is the bi-polar energy flowing through the temple system (see Figure 29). All this confirms the part played by the High Priest, in this case Aaron and his sons.

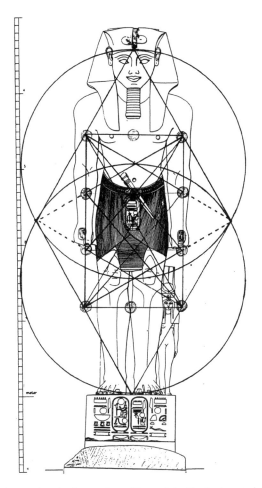

Figure 29. Pharaoh wearing the breastplate. Pharaoh holds the breastplate at the second row of jewels, whose position is determined by the major wholetone and the centre of the breastplate is at the level of his first Chakra. the base of the spine. The lower edge is at the level of the Queen's mouth. This confirms her dominant role in the creative process, which is sustained by the massive figure of the Pharaoh, hunched under the weight of the physical world.

Figure 29 shows a frontal view of the Pharaoh standing in the south corner of the Outer Court at Luxor, which we have already seen from the side (Figure 28). Here we see him in his priestly role, contained, as before, within the interlocking circles of fusion with diameters of 555 feet. He is wearing the breastplate with its twelve jewels, placed so that its musical proportions fit with those of the body. The higher energy enters the

Pharaoh's crown at C, is polarised, the "fine twined or twinned, linen" and flows through the system, setting up harmonic resonance between his body and the jewels of the breastplate, which then, in turn, resonate with the temple and are radiated out into the surroundings. This is the essential role of the Pharaoh, linking heaven and earth. The Queen (Mother and Wife) can be seen to the right and partly hidden by his left leg. Figure 28, showing the Pharaoh from the side, reveals that she has her right hand resting lightly on the back of his left calf. The tips of her fingers touch KL. For all the massive strength suggested by the male figure, it is that gentlest, but strongest energy, love, expressed by the Mother/Wife that flows into the system through her fingertips, softening and balancing the massive physicality expressed by the figure of the Pharaoh.

Figure 30 shows the young Pharaoh standing before Amon.[8] The same circles of fusion and their derived musical proportions have been superimposed.

This bas-relief is located in the temple at Luxor, in the Covered Temple, under the lintel of the door from Room XI; into the Inner Sanctuary, at the southwest end of the Temple. As shown in Figure 29, with the human body superimposed on the Temple plan, this is the position of the pituitary gland, which lies in the floor of the brain. De Lubicz refers to the part played by the pituitary and the growth of the long bones. A horizontal joint in the stonework links the god's eyes to the young Pharaoh's pituitary and a vertical joint links the horizontal one to his knees, confirming the pituitary's role in the growth of the long bones and hence in his height at maturity and the establishment of Pharaonic proportions in his realm. Through the link suggested with the god, we see the latter directing this process of harmonious growth. The relief suggests that the boy is the trunk of the tree and its leaves and branches indicate the life force, expressed as higher vibrations in the figure of the god and transposed by the Pharaoh into the three-dimensional world.

We saw that the Salmon (Solomon, Absalom etc.) are tree deities in the Osirian tradition. In Figure 30 the young Pharaoh holds what Schwaller de Lubicz refers to as "the fruits of the Persée plant". However, what he is actually suggesting is that the tree is associated with Perseus was "put in a wooden box and thrown into the sea", i.e. both Osiris and Perseus are tree deities.[9] This confirms that the young Pharaoh is in the Osirian tradition of tree deities, like the Hebrew Salmon.

This relief at the entrance to the Inner Sanctuary shows Amon directing creative energy from his Ankh, held in his left hand, through the fruit which Pharaoh holds in his right hand, to his navel, which is at

Figure 30. Young Pharaoh before Amon. Pharaoh essentially is the tree, the pomegranate, the sacred temple tree. Amon, on his right. directs creative energy from the Ankh in his left hand, through the pomegranate fruit in Pharaoh's right hand, into his third Chakra. With his right hand Amon writes on the two fruits, here shown as Aleph and Tav.

the centre 0 in vesica ABEF. This contains the seed which completes the cycle of birth, growth and death which is symbolised by Osiris. It also refers to the two circles of fusion, which combine Yin and Yang, 1080 + 666, to give 1746, the gematria of 'kokkos sinapeos', the mustard seed, symbolic of the Kingdom of Heaven, which is sustained by the deity. The life energy "passes through the seal on the buckle at the front of Pharaoh's belt, which depicts his 'name', his essence, his ability to link with his higher self and therefore the collective consciousness".

71

In his right hand Amon holds a stylus, which cuts through the peel of the fruit to the red rind, thereby tracing letters in red on the fruit.

The red colour revealed by the stylus is a clue of immense importance: it suggests that it is a pomegranate fruit, which has a red rind. This is *Punica malum*, the Phoenician apple, the Temple Tree. The red flowers have seven petals, a very unusual feature. It consists of a small genus that is so unlike any other orders of flowering plants that it is often put in a separate order, Granateae. The Greek name for pomegranate is 'sidē', whose gematria is 222 ($= 37 \times 6$). This is also the gematria of Ibis, the white wading bird which is often used to represent Thoth, the God of Writing, in Egyptian art.

Here we have Amon in the role of Thoth, inscribing Aleph and Tav, the first and last letters of the old Hebrew AlephBayt on the two pomegranates being presented by the Pharaoh. These are the two untranslated letters at the centre of the first verse of the first chapter of Genesis, the initiating impulse of creative energy from which the whole creation grows. As we know (see Figure 18), the first verse of Genesis and the Menorah (the six-branched candlestick) is represented as an almond tree in Hebrew mythology and this corresponds to the pomegranate in this Egyptian version of the creative process. As St. John puts it in the first verse of his Gospel, "In the beginning was the word" and here we see the god writing that creative word.

A ray of energy is transmitted from the stylus in the god's right hand, through both the fruits held by the Pharaoh, to K in the rectangle JKLM. As we know, this rectangle is part of the Metacube, of which the middle cube is the $2 \times 2 \times 2$ cube containing the twenty-seven letters of the Hebrew AlephBayt. Through this energy pathway we can see how St. John's paraphrase of Genesis 1:1 "... and the word was God..." is expressed in the 27-letter cube.

Schwaller de Lubicz[10] describes the Ankh as the "Key of Life" and we see it here transmitting creative energy from Amon's left hand, through the Pharaoh and into the tree, symbolising the physical world. Conventionally it is referred to as the "ansated cross", where 'ansated' is from the French 'une anse' (handle, of a basket etc.), referring to the loop with which Amon holds it. However, if we follow BC, one of the sides of the rhombus ABCD, this passes through the goose hieroglyph above the left-hand cartouche, in the tree above Pharaoh's head and 'anser' in Latin means 'goose', suggesting a link with the Ankh. As the goose appears here, together with a circle representing the Sun, it means "Son of the Sun" and we know that that is exactly what the Salmon is (Son o' Man/Solomon) in the Hebrew tradition, confirming that the latter is in the Egyptian Pharaonic tradition. This suggests that 'ansated' is a pun, indicating that Pharaoh uses the Ankh as a link to the Sun, in the sense of 'the Source of Life'.

Above the right-hand cartouche are two hieroglyphs: the one on the right has the appearance of a flag, or perhaps an axe. This is the Egyptian term 'Neter', meaning 'creative principle', which is being expressed here by Amon, through the Pharaoh. The musical proportions have been extended into the next octave, to $X'Y'$, the major wholetone ratio JM:JX' (8:9), indicating that the musical proportions underlying the whole Cosmic Scheme originate with the Creative Source, or deity, with the hieroglyph for Neter at X'. An example in Greek is the word kuboneter, the origin of the English word 'governor' meaning literally 'Principle of the Cube', where the 'cube' symbolises the three-dimensional world.

Robert and Deborah Lawlor[11] show the hieroglyph for Neter rotated through ninety degrees:

Here the distance from elbow to fingertips = 18 inches or 1 ell (hence ell.bow, demonstrated when the arm is bent, or 'bowed'). In Greek 'elbow' is ēōlēnē, whose gematria is 901 and the Hebrew word Shem 'name' (Sheen Final Mem) is 900, hence the deity's 'name' is imprinted on the creation through this measure, the ell, or biblical cubit of one foot six inches. In Figure 30, Amon's right arm holding the stylus is bent at right angles, as in the above drawing, and the distance from elbow to fingertips is equal to the distance EF, the radius of the two interlocking circles, 3 feet on the scale of the body of the adult Pharaoh, as shown in Figure 29, the Pharaoh superimposed on the temple plan. This gives a total height for the adult Pharaoh of 9 feet. $1\frac{1}{2}$ feet being equal to 18 inches, this equals 2×9 and the gematria of the Hebrew 'cubit' Aleph Mem Hay is 46, while $45 = 5 \times 9$, confirming the link between the Ell and the Biblical Cubit.

In the English translations of the Old Testament, the Hebrew word 'shem' is usually translated as 'name', as in "David gat him a name",[12] but this doesn't make sense, since he already had a name. The Hebrew word shemen, translated as 'ointment', 'savour' and 'oil', has the same root, Sheen Final Mem, and all these are associated with the act of 'crowning' or 'enthroning' and just as Jedidiah was made Solomon,[13] i.e. he was initiated as the Salmon or priest-king, so was David in being 'named'. This Hebrew word Shem comes from the Egyptian word tcham, whose general meaning is 'sceptre', which is a symbol of the priest-king's power and authority and is probably derived from the Ankh. Thus the Pharaoh's name, displayed in the two cartouches in the pome-granate tree, contains the figure of the deity holding an Ankh and other symbols of power. The ray of energy BC, radiating from Amon's Ankh, passes through the feet of the deity in the right-hand cartouche and this point forms a major centre in the musical proportions shown in the drawing. For example, MY, indicating the major wholetone, passes through Pharaoh's mouth and larynx (at E), suggesting that Amon is directing the creative sounds coming from Pharaoh.

At this point we need to look again at Bond and Lea's diagram illustrating the Cabala of the Fish.[14] They base this on intersecting circles whose radius is 704 ($= 37 \times 20$, the gematria of the "Concept of Truth" etc.). The resulting vesica piscis, ABEF, has a long axis AB of 1219 ($= 704 \times \sqrt{3}$). But this is also the gematria of the Greek Sothis, the star Sirius and this lifts the whole discussion out of the Christian, New Testament level, to a cosmic one. Furthermore, Bond and Lea state that "the area of the greater rhombus (ABCD) is 1288"[15] the gematria of 'o ichthys', the fish. Again the cosmic nature underlying the Cabala is revealed by the fact that Osiris written in Greek as Osothis, has this gematria of 1289; so that the whole Cabala is based on the Sirius star system expressed in the Egyptian pantheon as Isis and Osiris. As we already know, it is the amphibious being Oannes, the origin of the ritual of Baptism, who is the fish, represented in the diagram of the Cabala of the Fish, who is depicted as the vesica ABEF. Temple[16] presents a detailed case for Oannes having come from Sirius. In Sumerian myth he is depicted as having taught Mankind the arts of civilisation. I believe he did more than this: he imprinted the geometry of our Cosmic Scheme and that of Bond and Lea's Cabala on the crystalline/atomic structure of our planet.

Temple[17] discusses the nature of the Egyptian word 'Tcham', which seems to refer to the sceptre as an instrument of power, similar to the Ankh. It is "a kind of precious metal" and perhaps the sceptre is made from it. Wallis Budge quotes from the Pyramid Texts, referring to the deceased Pharaoh Pepi: "various gods, including the Governor of the Land of the Bow and Sept (Sir-ius) carry a ladder for Pepi". Here the Governor of the Bow sounds very like our Lord of the Bow, Amon with his arm bent, or 'bowed', directing the process of creation through the young Pharaoh and we have the explicit link with Sirius. The specific use of the term 'Governor', which we know comes from the term 'Kubon Neter', "Principle of the Cube", Creator of the physical world, confirms the link with Amon in Figure 30.

Temple, quoting Wallis Budge again, writes "Pepi stands among the imperishable stars, which stand upon their tcham sceptres" referring again to the sceptres made of this mysterious metal of immense strength, notes that the Greeks have a tradition of 'the strongest metal' and call it 'adamant', adamas, hence our word adamantine. Returning to the links with Sirius, the bright star, known as Sirius A, has a dark twin, Sirius B, which as we saw in connection with the fifty-year Jubilee, orbits its bright neighbour every fifty years. This is a senescent star, which has collapsed inwards to form a body of immense density, in which one thimble-full is equal to the mass of our whole Earth. The Egyptian word 'tchens', meaning 'weight', Temple suggests is linked with 'tcham'. The association of the deity's sceptre with tcham indicates a very effective symbolism, suggesting the immense power of the deity expressed through the sceptre, Ankh etc.

So, when David "gat him a name",[18] he was initiated into the secrets of the role of the priest-king, as intermediary between Earth and the higher planes of life. Essentially, it is this initiation which we see Pharaoh undergoing as he stands before Amon in Figure 30. Likewise, when David in his turn "called his name Solomon",[19] he was initiating his son. The Hebrew text has Aleph Tav-Sheen Mem Vav Sheen Lammed Mem Hay where Sheen Mem Vav is the name, or tcham. The gematria of Sheen Lammed Mem Hay (Solomon) is 375 and $4 \times 375 = 1500$, the gematria of light, which fits with his role as the Sun o' Man. In the next verse David "called his name Jedidiah", using the same term Sheen Mem, "for the Lord's sake". But this last phrase in the Hebrew is Bayt Ayn Bayt Vav Raish Yod Hay Vav Hay, whose gematria is 306 and $2 \times 306 = 612$, the gematria of Zeus, suggesting that David is initiating his son into the role of a god. In the Hebrew Jedidiah is Yod Dallet Yod Dallet Yod Hay, whose gematria is 43, the seventh of Bond and Lea's formative numbers and the last prime number in Plichter's second ring of 24 (see Figure 14). This number "raised by the power of Ten, is the number of nomos (the Law), and of Number itself (arithmos). And this number ... controls, unites and harmonises the measures of circles and rectilinear figures in a manner that no other simple number could do".[20] Some idea of what Bond and Lea are suggesting is given when 430 is multiplied by $\sqrt{3}$, giving 744, which is equal to 31×24, the second and third rings and centre of their Metacube,[21] so that it embodies both the $2 \times 2 \times 2$ cube of the 27 Hebrew letters and the $4 \times 4 \times 4$ cube with its 64 points, 64×24 being 1536, the gematria of the True Geometry in Greek.

744 is also the gematria of the Greek Theotokos, 'The Offspring of God', which the Pharaoh/Salmon clearly is. Bond and Lea point out that:

$$\text{'Parthenos' (virgin)} = 515$$

$$\underline{\text{'o aner' (the man)} = 229}$$

$$744$$

"the union of the two principles". This is exactly what we have in Figure 30, the young Pharaoh before Amon, where the intersecting circles whose diameters are 555, have a circumference of 1746 ($\pi \times 555 = 1746$), and the masculine and feminine; $666 + 1080 = 1746$, 'kokkos sinapeos', the grain of mustard seed. 744 is also the gematria of 'ē Mētēr Semelē' (the Mother Semele), "spouse of Zeus; who gives birth to Dionysos, whose name is a clever anagram of Nous Dios, the Mind of Zeus". But we have already seen that the phrase translated into English as "for the Lord's sake" has gematria 306, 2×306 being equal to 612, the gematria of Zeus, suggesting that David is initiating his son into the role of a god.[22] So one outcome of the Shem (initiation) is that the masculine and feminine polarity expressed in the human personality is brought into balance and fused into one.

Returning to Temple,[23] he says "Concerning this star metal (tcham)... Plutarch says of the Egyptians, 'Moreover, they call the lodestone the bone of Horus, and iron the bone of Typhon', as Manetho records. ... It is interesting that a heavy metal is 'the bone' of Typhon, which we have earlier determined as a description of Sirius B". As we know, 'sideros' (iron) and 'sideretes' (the lodestone) have the root 'side', pomegranate in Greek. All this seems to be suggesting some link between the pomegranate and the enormously heavy metal tcham. The first clue is in Exodus 28:33: "And thou shalt make (the robe of the Ephod) upon its skirts, pomegranates of blue, and of purple, and of scarlet...and bells of gold between them". Here we have the four colours of the jewels of the Salmon's magic ring, which we know refer to the four elements/four fundamental forces and it is red which is the key: on the one hand it is the colour of the flowers and juice of the pomegranate and of the rind of its fruit which is revealed when Amon writes the two letters embodying the Creative Energies on it; on the other hand it is the colour of the jewel in the magic ring which refers to the fundamental force gravity. So Pharaoh, as the trunk of the pomegranate tree, embodies the enormous weight of tcham and carries it in his sceptre, the symbol of his power before the world. Figures 29 and 30 show the Pharaoh hunched under the weight of the temple structure, graphically expressing his role in sustaining the three-dimensional universe. However, behind the massive figure of the Pharaoh stands the slender figure of the Queen, Mother and Wife, lightly resting her hand on the back of his calf, reminding us that it is in this strongest but gentlest of forces, love, that the real art of creation lies.

Regarding the 'colours' in the Hebrew text, we arrive at a most extraordinary discovery: in Exodus 26:1 we have "Moreover thou shalt make the tabernacle with ten curtains, ... blue and purple, and scarlet ... the work of a cunning workman ...". The first indication of the profound nature of this passage is the term 'cunning workman', which, as we know, indicates that the passage is referring to cosmic creative processes. We also know that the colours refer to the four fundamental forces of modern physics, weak nuclear force, which operates in the formation of stars, strong nuclear force, which holds the nuclei of atoms together, electromagnetism and gravity. In the Hebrew text, the gematria of "and blue, and purple, and scarlet" is:

$$
\begin{array}{rr}
\text{blue} = & 856 \\
\text{purple} = & 950 \\
\text{scarlet} = & \underline{912} \\
& 2718.0
\end{array}
$$

As Bond and Lea show,[24] it is the numbers that are significant, not the position of the decimal point. In this example, by moving the point three places to the left, we get the number 2.718. Remarkably, this is Euler's number.[25] Its appearance here in the gematria of the Hebrew text could be dismissed as due to chance. However, the colours whose gematria make up the total in gematria of 2718 refer to the three fundamental forces, respectively blue, purple and red, weak nuclear force, strong nuclear force and gravity, suggesting that the writers knew about the Euler constant and its significance with regard to the fundamental forces.

Plichta shows a table of the 81 stable elements. "There are elements with several stable forms, or isotopes (and) we may liken an element with isotopes to a family with children. No matter how many children there are, the family remains the family. So an element remains that element no matter how many isotopes it has".

"Yet although greater numbers of children in a family are not unknown, one element can have an absolute maximum of ten isotopes".

"Nobody knows why this is so. . . . It is necessary to point out that we are deliberately kept in the dark about the fact that there can be no more than ten isotopes because the number ten appears a bit too mystical for some people in high places".[26]

Verses 1 and 2 of Exodus 26 refer to 'ten curtains' and, given what we now know about the rest of verse 1, it seems likely that 'ten' may refer to this maximum of ten isotopes and the Hebrew for 'curtains' is Tav Ayn Sheen Hay, whose gematria is 775 and $777 = 37 \times 21$, which, according to Bond and Lea, is the gematria of the Greek 'stauros', 'cross'[27].

Assuming that the cross is an equal-armed Celtic cross, rather than the Roman cross associated with the Crucifixion, we now come to a reference to another of Bligh Bond's works, *The Gate of Remembrance*.[28] Here Bond shows a plan of Glastonbury Abbey based on a grid of 74-foot squares. His Figure 4, the four-petalled lotus, shows two pairs of intersecting circles, with centres at E and F and G and H. These intersect at J, K, L and M, giving the square JKLM. The dimensions of the figure and the relevant gematria are:

AB and CD = 153 feet, the fishes in the net in John 21

EF = 88 feet, the gematria of Thoth, the Egyptian Hermes.

JKLM has sides of 74 feet ($= 2 \times 37$), the gematria of the Hebrew Ayn Dallet, the root of the Hebrew word for 'time' and 74 feet is equal to 888 inches ($= 37 \times 24$), the gematria of Jesus in Greek. The area of the square JKLM is 740 square megalithic yards (MY), and $740 = 37 \times 20$, and is the gematria of a complex of Greek words, including 'ktisis' (creation) and 'kyklos' (cycle) and the Hebrew Jakin, one of the two main pillars of the Temple.

All this shows how the different creative energies, under the names of deities and other significant words and phrases, expressed in the gematria, combine to make a geometric pattern, which manifests as physical form, in this case Glastonbury Abbey.

In Figure 4 of *The Gate of Remembrance*, the equal armed cross is made by AB and CD, each having a length of 153 and $2 \times 153 = 306$, while $2 \times 306 = 612$, the gematria of Zeus. But 88, the gematria of Thoth, multiplied by 4 is 352 and the gematria of Hermes is 353 and $353 \times \sqrt{3} = 612$ confirming that the geometry on which the plan is built and the Abbey itself, is a manifestation of a complex of higher energies. John Michell[29] shows the same diagram and states that "This same figure has recently been published in T. C. Stewart's *The City as an Image of Man* as the Founding of Indian Temple from Manasara Shilpa Shastra, which describes the Vedic method for orientating and laying out of temple plans".

10

THE FOUR COLOURS

Returning to the significance of the four colours in the furnishings of the Tabernacle and the High Priest's robes, one colour, gold, stands apart from the other three, blue, purple and scarlet. While these last three all have gematria with high numbers, 856, 950 and 912 respectively, the word translated as gold in Hebrew, Zayn Hay Bayt, has the unusually low number of 14. Is there any significance in this difference?

The answer lies in the number fourteen itself. In his Table 1, Plichta shows the element carbon as having $2 + 1$ isotopes. Its atomic weight is 12, but one of these isotopes has the atomic weight 14 and is known as C_{14}. It is radioactive and, although it occurs at very low concentrations, it is present in all organic compounds and particularly in all living organisms. C_{14} occurs so widely because it is present in carbon dioxide (CO_2) in the air. It is then combined with water, in the process of photosynthesis to form glucose and other carbohydrates and then proteins etc. in the structure of the plant. The plants are then eaten and assimilated by animals, so that the C_{14} is present in all animal tissues.

In this way solar energy is converted into chemical energy and forms the basis for all life on Earth. Since the fourth fundamental force, the yellow jewel in the Salmon's ring, is an electromagnetic force, this fits with the Sun as the source of such a force. It also fits with the symbolism of the Pharaoh/Salmon as the Sun o' Man (Sol-o'-Mon), the "Being like unto the Sun" at the centre of the Menorah in Chapter 1 of Revelation. David established the royal house, leading down through Jedediah (Solomon) to Jesus and they were of the tribe of Judah which Villalpanda shows as corresponding astrologically to the Lion, which is ruled by the Sun. Is it a coincidence that the gematria of David, Dallet, Vav Dallet, like 'gold', has the unusually low value of 14?

One of the Salmon's four jewels in his magic ring is described as a lion and one of Ezekiel's four 'creatures' had "the face of a lion".

Ezekiel continues: "...one wheel...for each of the four faces there-of...their appearance...(was) as it were a wheel within a wheel...they four (creatures) had their rings full of eyes round about".[1]

All this suggests orbiting bodies, where the 'wheels' are orbits, "an orbit within an orbit" and the eyes are, for example, electrons in an atom. In view of this, it is perhaps not so surprising that the writers of the Hebrew text should know the difference between ^{12}C and its radioactive isotope, C_{14}. As we saw, this points to a link with the four 'colours', gold and electromagnetism, one of the four fundamental forces. The isotope C_{14}, like all radioactive substances, shows a decline in radioactivity in accordance with Euler's number of 2.718.

In the Hebrew text 'creatures' is written as Hay Hhayt Yod Vav Tav, whose gematria is 429 and 430 is the gematria of Nomos, the Law "and of Number itself – Arithmos".[2] This is in remarkable conformity with the fact that Euler's number is involved with radioactive decay and therefore with the two fundamental forces concerned with radioactivity and with the force of gravity, in determining the rate of decline in gravitational force with altitude and now with C_{14} and the Sun and hence with electro-magnetic force". And why this number is chosen for the purpose of symbolising the controlling factor is, on geometric grounds, quite clear, and capable of satisfactory proof, but all that can here be said is that it controls, unites and harmonises the measures of circles and rectilinear figures in a manner that no other simple number could do". Now we can see that, through the gematria of 'creatures' in Hebrew, this number operates in sustaining the whole physical world through the operation of the four fundamental forces, a concept unknown when Bond and Lea were writing. The whole field of quantum mechanics, hinted at in Ezekiel's 'wheels' and 'eyes' and about to be published when our authors were writing, was unknown to them. How much more is there hidden in the Hebrew text and waiting to be revealed? One example of this concerns one of the four fundamental forces, that of gravity. Physics has still not discovered the nature of gravitational force, a gravi-tron, a gravity particle. Yet, this must exist. If it does not, then the whole framework of modern physics collapses.

Are there any hints in the Hebrew text that might suggest that the writers knew something about the nature of gravity that we have not redis-covered? They were clearly well aware of the concept of weight and mass. As we know, the Hebrew 'Shem' is derived from the Egyptian 'Tcham'; with its allusion to the immense density of the star Sirius B. We also saw that both the Greek words 'sidēros' (iron) and 'sidērētēs' (the lodestone), have the root 'sidē', pomegranate, hinting at a link between the latter and

the concept of gravity. The gematria of sidē is 222, which is also the gematria of the Hebrew Kaf Raysh Bayt, ch-r-b, or 'cherub'. "And every one
had four faces: the first face was the face of a cherub, and the second face
was the face of a man, and the third the face of a lion, and the forth the
face of an eagle".[3] Here, by elimination, we can establish which of the
four 'faces', or forces, is represented by the cherubim. We know that 'a
man' and 'an eagle' refer to the two kinds of nuclear radiation and that
the lion corresponds to the electromagnetic force, so that the cherubim
refer to gravity, as does the pomegranate, which has the same gematria.
"For the cherubim spread forth their wings over the place of the ark. . . .
And it came to pass, when the priests were come out of the holy place,
that the cloud filled the house of the Lord, so that the priests could not
stand to minister by reason of the cloud".[4]

The 'cloud' refers to the immense energy field being emitted by the
ark and the fact that the priests 'could not stand' indicates its enormous
power. We know that the cherubim symbolise the force of gravity and
this passage indicates its great strength. We also know that the observance
of the fifty-year Jubilee cycle recognises the fifty-year period of the orbit
of Sirius B round Sirius A, and, by implication, the fluctuating gravitational field emitted by Sirius B and its influence on the Earth. The
reason why modern physics cannot detect this force and measure it is
that suitable instruments have not been designed, not because it is too
weak to have a perceptible effect from eight light years' distance. The
physics establishment is concerned because it cannot find evidence for
the existence of a gravity particle; yet it refuses to look outside the bound-
aries of its own discipline and therefore is unable to solve the problem.

". . . and the people piped with pipes . . . so that the earth rent with
the sound of them".[5] We have seen the power emitted by the sound of
the wings of the cherubim and, since the cherubim symbolise the fundamental force of gravity, the rending of the earth by 'pipes', i.e. by sound
produced by musical instruments, is further evidence that suggests a link
between gravity and sound. In the Hebrew text, the word translated in
the English version as 'pipes' is Hhayt Lammed Lammed, Hilel, a
sound produced by the human voice. In Welsh it is the Hywel, the
tribal cry produced by a crowd in order to intimidate the enemy. The
English version is 'howl', a loud discordant sound. In "rending the
earth", the sounding of the Hilel is shown to be a destructive sound,
derived from its discordant nature.

"In his days did Hiel . . . build Jericho".[6] In using a capital H for Hiel,
the translators are suggesting that it is a personal name, but it is written in
the Hebrew as Hhayt Yod Aleph Lammed, which is very similar to Hilel.

Therefore Hiel, being associated with building, suggests the use of sound to achieve a positive result, while the Hilel is used for destruction. Hiel has gematria of 49 (7^2) and we shall see that this has a profound significance in relation to Jericho.

"And the Lord said unto Joshua, see, I have given into thy hand Jericho".[7] The gematria of Jericho is 240 and $240 \times 2/5 = 48$, while that of the sound energy used to build it, the Hiel, is 49.

"And ye shall compass the city, all the men of war; going about the city once. Thus shalt thou do six days. And seven priests shall bear seven trumpets of rams' horns before the ark: and the seventh day ye shall compass the city seven times, and the priests shall blow with the trumpets. And it shall be, that when they make a long blast with the rams' horn, and when ye hear the sound of the trumpet, all the people shall shout with a great shout; and the wall of the city shall fall down flat".[8]

The first indication as to what is really going on here concerns the trumpets: the 1885 translation gives 'jubile trumpets' as an alternative to 'rams' horns' and the Hebrew text has Yod Vav Bayt Lammed, 'jubile'. So what is so special about 'jubile trumpets'? The first part of the answer lies in the nature of the trumpets, which, unlike modern instruments, would not have valves and would therefore only be capable of playing one harmonic series. This suggests that these trumpets were designed with a particular and unusual harmonic system in mind.

The second part of the answer lies in the gematria: the word 'jubile' in Hebrew has the gematria 48 and in verse 4 above we have "Seven priests shall bear seven trumpets" and "the seventh day ye shall compass the city seven times", suggesting 7×7, or 49 and we already know that the gematria of Jericho is $240 \times 2/5$, and $240 \times 2/5$ is equal to 48. Furthermore, we also know that the orbital period of Sirius B round Sirius A is 49 years, so that, rather than being concerned with a tribal war, the text is trying to convey information about the Sirius system and, in particular, about Sirius B. We know about the intense gravitational force emitted by Sirius B and that the jubile period of 49/50 years was established to harmonise with variations in these emissions during this orbital period. The circuits around the "walls of Jericho" appear to be enacting the observance of the jubile year and the playing of the jubile trumpets at intervals which fit with the appropriate stages in the Sirian orbital period, culminating with the 'great shout', suggest that a resonant field was being built up, leading to a blast of sound, the Hilel, which knocked down the walls of the city.

All this was taking place during the Israelite conquest of Canaan and the gematria of the latter in Greek is 703 ($= 37 \times 19$), suggesting that the conquest is really a cosmic process. The phrase in Hebrew, translated as "shout with a great shout", has the gematria 1702, which is equal to 37×46, another example of a multiple of the prime number 37, which fits into Bond and Lea's series and confirms the cosmic significance of the siege of Jericho.

There are many archaeological examples, such as the Great Pyramid and Stonehenge, where ramps, rafts and rollers are involved to give a 'rational' explanation for the movement of megaliths and one which allows us to go on believing that people in the past could not possibly have known more than we do. These examples of the constructive use of sound to control the force of gravity are, I believe, evidence of the use of a technique similar to that described being used at Jericho. In the latter case, Hiel, positive, constructive sound was used to build the city and Hilel, negative, destructive sound was used to destroy it.

"And when the Ark of the Covenant of the Lord came into the camp, all Israel shouted with a great shout, so that the earth rang again".[9] Most people reading this would regard the expression "the earth rang" as an example of poetic licence, but in view of what we have seen regarding the events at Jericho, it seems reasonable to take this statement literally. We know that our planet is within the gravitational field of the Sirius system and that the Israelite priesthood understood how to control and direct this immense force for both constructive and destructive purposes. In the Hebrew text the term "ark of the covenant" has the gematria 1519 and $1517 = 37 \times 41$, the gematria of the Greek 'ē archē kosmou', 'the beginning of the kosmos'. The English term 'ark' comes from the Greek 'archē' and the Hebrew ark is, in the profoundest sense, the beginning, or creative source of the whole kosmos.

"The Ark of the Covenant dwelleth between the cherubim".[10] In the Hebrew text "dwelleth between" has the gematria of 499, the same as the Greek 'thronos' (throne), and we know that this refers to 0, the centre of the cosmic scheme. We can now locate the ark and cherubim within the scheme. The ark is the vesica with its long axis EF and the cherubim are placed on each side, at L' and K'. The unipolar gravitational force entering the system at C is polarised by the pillars Jakin and Boaz, at K and L. It then flows around the ark to the cherubim at K' and L', building a polarised gravitational field between them, in the ark.

The importance of strictly maintaining this layout, the spatial relationship between the temple pillars and the ark, is demonstrated when "the ark of God was taken" by the Philistines. "The glory is departed from Israel".[11] In other words, the life-giving energies radiating out to the Israelites were lost. In taking the ark from the temple complex, the whole creative system was disrupted. The effects of this disruption are demonstrated by the misfortunes suffered by the Philistines while the ark was in their possession: "And the Philistines took the ark of God . . . and set it by Dagon (their god) and . . .". next morning "Dagon was fallen on his face". They tried again and this time "Dagon was fallen upon his face before the ark . . ." and the head of Dagon and both his hands lay cut off upon the threshold".[12]

But this was only the beginning of the misfortunes suffered by the Philistines while they had the ark: "But the hand of the Lord was heavy upon them . . . and he smote them and destroyed them with tumours" (verse 6). This sounds very like the effects of exposure to nuclear radiation. Looking again at Figure 6, we know that the four jewels/creatures etc. are concerned with the four fundamental forces and two of these are forms of nuclear force. The experiences of the Philistines suggests that the ark had to be correctly placed within the temple system, as shown in the figure, to keep the radiation under control. The damage to Dagon suggests that the gravitational force was out of balance, in the same way as the nuclear forces.

The Philistines, in desperation, took the ark from place to place, but wherever they took it, "tumours brake out upon them" (verse 10), ". . . and they said, send away the ark of the God of Israel, and let it go again to its own place" (verse 12). This suggests that they had realised that it was essential for the ark to be correctly placed to enable it to function in a creative way. Poussin's painting *La Peste d'Azoth* shows the ark abandoned half out of the temple, lying between the two pillars, Jakin and Boaz. All around people are dying from the effects of the plague and the artist makes the link between the plague and the position of the ark very clear. As we have already seen in connection with Jericho, Hiel and Hilel refer to the positive constructive and the negative/destructive aspects of this immensely powerful system. Here we have an example of the destructive effects of the system in the wrong hands.

In their efforts to escape the effects of the ark in their midst, the Philistines shuffle it round their five cities and there were "five lords of the Philistines".[13] When they returned the ark they made a guilt offering of "five golden tumours and five golden mice, according to the number of the lords of the Philistines".[14] All this makes a contrast with the association of the Israelites with the number seven and its multiple 49: the gematria of Hiel (= 49) and of Jubile (= 48), the seven priests, trumpets and circuits of the walls of Jericho and the 49 year orbit of Sirius B. These relate to the Sirian gravitational system and suggest that the latter is based on harmonics of 7. This is demonstrated in Figure 29, the statue of the Pharaoh and his

Table 4.

Harmonic	Frequency (Hz)	Body of Pharoah	Temple plan
C	66	Top of head	Inner wall
c	132	Larynx, top of shoulder	–
g	198	Base of sternum	Pillars, Hypostyle hall
c′	264	Base of spine	–
e	330	Thumb and knuckles	–
g′	396	Back of knee	Entrance to Colonnade
b′ flat	462	Base of Queen's spine	
c″	528	Sole of Queen's foot	Other side of entrance

mother/wife superimposed on the plan of the temple at Luxor. Here the width of the Covered Temple gives the base note of 44 megalithic yards (1 MY = 2.72 feet or 0.829 metres). $7 \times 44 = 308$ and this is expressed as seven harmonics of 44, extending through three octaves, from two octaves below middle c, to one octave above.

In *Le Temple de l'Homme*, Schwaller de Lubicz relates stages in the growth of the human body to stages in the building of the temple, with, for example, the Covered Temple being 2/7ths of the total length, the first part to be built and the height of a new-born child having a height equal to 2/7ths of the height of the adult. The whole process of growth forms a harmonic series, with the base note sounded at birth and the harmonics marking successive stages in development (see Figure 31). Stages in the development of the building follow this same harmonic series. Essentially, this is what gives a building, such as a temple, or church, a feeling of sacredness, since its proportions resonate harmoniously with those of the bodies of people inside it.

Returning to the conflict between the Israelites and the Philistines, the prevalence of the number 5 in relation to the latter suggests a different, pentatonic vibrational basis, in contrast to the diatonic system of the Israelites, one with five intervals per octave, the other with seven. The result of the confrontation between the ark and Dagon and the plague which the Philistines suffered while they had the ark in their possession, may have been caused by a conflict between two gravitational systems, each based on different harmonics and which gave rise to a discordant result when they were brought together.

"And [David]...chose him five smooth stones...and put them in the shepherd's bag which he had...and his sling was in his hand.... And

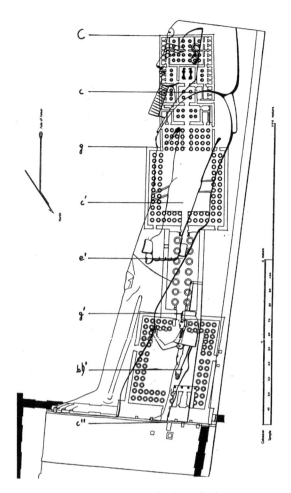

Figure 31. Pharaoh and the temple plan: the harmonics.

David put his hand in his bag, and took thence a stone, and slang it, and smote [Goliath] in his forehead"[15] (1 Samuel 17:40 and 49).

Here we have five cropping up again, suggesting that in slinging the stones at Goliath, David's seven-based harmonics were strong enough to reflect Goliath's five-based ones back at him. The Hebrew word translated as 'stones' is Aleph Bayt Nun Yod Final Mem and its gematria is 663, hinting at 666, which is equal to 37×18, the gematria of the Greek Teitan, which fits with Goliath's great size. In addition, 'smooth' is Hhayt Lammed KQof Yod, 148 in gematria, 37×4, confirming the cosmic significance of the text.

In the phrase "David put his hand in his bag", the gematria of 'David', 'hand' and 'bag' are respectively 14, 20 and 65 and $14 + 20 + 65 = 99$ and $98 = 7 \times 14$, suggesting a harmonic series based on 7. Then, with slight changes, we have the series as follows:

$$14, 21, 63, \quad \text{or } 2 \times 7, 3 \times 7, 9 \times 7.$$

This indicates that David embodies the harmonic system of the whole of Israel, which fits with Saul's choice of David to represent the people against Goliath.

"...and (Goliath) fell upon his face to the earth",[16] and in 1 Samuel 5:3 we have "Dagon was fallen upon his face to the ground". Where the English text has 'ground' in one case and 'earth' in the other, the Hebrew word Aleph Raysh Tsadde Hay is used in both. So the encounter between David and Goliath is essentially the same in terms of the harmonics as that between the ark and Dagon and the battle is between two harmonic systems.

Figure 32 is reproduced from Robert Temple's book *The Sirius Mystery*, which he refers to as "an ancient Greek vase painting".[17] Near

Figure 32. This Greek vase painting shows an attack from the constellation of Orion on the Sirius star system. The warrior on the right represents Orion and the temple on the left represents Sirius.

the bottom edge of the picture are two representations of what Temple suggests are stars, indicating that the whole picture is concerned with conflict between constellations: the hare between the two stars being the constellation of that name and the warrior representing the constellation of Orion, which appears in the sky above the Hare. The serpent, to the left and below the warrior, is in the position of Sirius. Written in hieroglyphics, the goddess Sirius would be:

literally 'serpent's tooth'[18] and he draws attention to the prominent rows of teeth, not just fangs, in the serpent's mouth, confirming that it represents Sirius. The figure of the warrior fits perfectly with the impression we have of the heavily armed giant, Goliath, and he confirms the identity of the contestants when he says: "Am I a dog . . .",[19] by which he is clearly distinguishing himself and the constellation Orion, from the Dog star Sirius. Furthermore, 'Orion' in Hebrew is Kaf Samech Yod Lammed, whose gematria is 120, which is equal to 5×24, where 5 refers to the base note of the Philistine vibrational system. 'David', on the other hand, is 14 ($= 2 \times 7$), while the gravitational frequency of the Sirius system, established by the orbital period of Sirius B is 49, or 7×7. This is underlined by the serpent on the extreme left, which has seven coils in its body.

We now know that what is, on the surface, an inter-tribal affair in Canaan, is a cosmic battle between constellations. But can we establish the nature of the attack and what it is aimed at? The first thing to notice is the two pairs of birds, one on the temple roof and the other associated with the warrior on right. We know that two doves flew from Thebes in Egypt (Thebes from Phoenician 'thybun', navel), one to Dodona, the other to Siwa, to establish oracles and hence omphaloi.[20] These form a triangle, with one oracle centre at each corner, and the roof forms a triangle, with one dove on each side. If Thebes is the loop at the top, then the overhang of the eves on each side represent Dodona and Siwa, all indicating that the temple is an oracle centre. The vertical and horizontal lines on the left form a mesh and such patterns are associated with omphalos stones, including those at Delphi and Delos,[21] confirming that this represents an omphalos.

In chapter 8 of Genesis Noah releases a dove and a raven and the raven "flew to and fro".[22] In the Hebrew text, 'to and fro' is Vav Yod Tsadde Aleph Yod Tsadde Vav Aleph, 'Vetsava Etsava', onomatopoeic terms suggesting the to and fro movement of the shuttle in weaving. Hence the raven or 'black dove' is the 'flying shuttle', weaving the etheric fabric upon which the physical world is built. The gematria of the Hebrew Vetsava Etsava is $107 + 107$, which equals 214 and the gematria of the Hebrew Debir, the house of the oracle, or most holy place, is 216, confirming the link between the etheric net and the oracle centres, such as Delphi and Delos. Furthermore, the gematria of the Hebrew Hay Ayn Raysh Bayt (raven) is 277 and $2 \times 277 = 554$, while $555 = 37 \times 15$, the diameter of the interlocking circles in our cosmic scheme. In the network on the left of the vase painting there are 11 vertical lines and 19 horizontal ones and the ratio $11:19 = 1:\sqrt{3}$, expressing the relationship between one dimension, the side of the cube of Hebrew letters, and its internal diagonal, expressing three dimensions. It is this harmonic reduction in the frequencies of the higher creative energies, which takes place within the cosmic scheme, which gives rise to our three-dimensional world and the Sirian system, based on harmonics of 7. This is represented by the temple that is being challenged by the Orionian/Philistinian system based on harmonics of 5.

As we saw, the serpent on the left-hand side of the temple has seven loops in its body, referring to the seven-based nature of the Sirius system. This is emphasised by the two rows of small rectangles between the roof and the capital of the pillar: the lower row has eight and the upper one has nine rectangles, pointing to the $8:9$ ratio of the major wholetone in the diatonic octave, with its seven intervals.

"When Pharaoh shall speak unto you, saying, show a wonder... then thou shalt say unto Aaron, Take thy rod and cast it down before Pharaoh, that it become a serpent... and Aaron cast down his rod before Pharaoh, and it became a serpent".[23] Here, in Figure 32 we have the passive, neutral form of energy, the pillar, and the active alternating form, polarised between the positive and the negative, represented by the serpent coiled round it. As we know this is also the energy flowing through the cosmic scheme, from C to D (see Figure 23). Figure 33 shows the statue of Moses at the north door of Chartres Cathedral.[24] Moses is shown holding one of the tablets of the Law in his left hand. Out of the upper end of the tablet a pillar emerges, with a dragon emerging from the capital and its tail coiled around the shaft of the pillar.

The tablet has the shape and proportions of the choir of the cathedral, with the curved end of the apse uppermost. This is also the

Figure 33. Moses at Chartres. The statue of Moses at the north door of the cathedral. He holds a column and a tablet of the Law. A dragon, with its body wound around the column, emerges from the capital. The tablet has the same proportions as the plan of the choir of the cathedral.

shape of omphaloi.[25] The dimensions and orientation of the choir are determined by a neolithic long barrow, which was on the site three thousand years before the cathedral was built. Charpentier shows how the prehistoric mound was oriented to the equinoctial sunrise.[26] A chapel on the north side of the choir is dedicated to "Notre Dame du Pilier", Our Lady of the Pillar, a medieval reference to the pillar whose shadow was used to orient the original mound. The medieval sculptor was clearly aware of all this and has set out to put this Christian building into the tradition of the omphalos, the energy centre, in the choir, the equivalent of the Holy of Holies. The folds of Moses' robe sweep up to converge on a point on the tablet, which, in the plan of the choir, is opposite the chapel of Notre Dame du Pilier, the point of orientation where the omphalos was placed during the process of orientation of the long barrow.[27]

"And Moses...went down from the mount, with the two tables of the testimony in his hand; tables that were written on both their sides;

on the one side and on the other were they written".[28] The repetition indicates that the author is trying to communicate something of particular importance. This is confirmed by the gematria: "tables written on both...". in Hebrew has the gematria 1870 and $1872 = 128 \times 24$; 'tablet' is 804 and doubling this for the two tablets gives 1608, or 67×24, while 'sides' is 887, and $888 = 37 \times 24$, the three visible sides in Bond and Lea's $4 \times 4 \times 4$ cube.[29] I believe that "written on both sides" is meant to indicate that the 'writing' was not inscribed on the surface of the stone, but that what the author is trying to tell us is that the 'writing' refers to the atomic structure of the limestone itself, referring to the creative process in which the atomic patterns of the different substances which make up our world are determined by the resonance patterns within the cube of Hebrew letters, according to the energies of the letters composing the creative sound.

The 'mount' (Hebrew Hay Raysh, or 'hor') is composed of limestone rock and in Hebrew limestone is Sammekh Yod Dallet, whose gematria is 74 ($= 2 \times 37$). As we saw in the passage from Daniel 12:7 etc., "Time, times and half a time", the root of the Hebrew word for 'time' is Ayn Dallet, whose gematria is 74 (2×37), establishing the frequency of the Base note D, 37 Hz, in the two octave series D_1 ('half a time'), D ('time') and d ('times'). Here, in the substance of the tablets, whose crystalline structure epitomises the creative process in its atomic pattern, we have a reference to the vibrational basis of matter, the Law underlying all creation.

11

THE OMPHALOS

The omphalos (Om Phalos, or world navel), goes back to the very beginning of creation, since there can be no physical manifestation until a link has been made between the higher creative energies and the dense level of the three dimensions. It begins with the Shemsu Hor, the initiates of the mound, in Egyptian records. Here 'shem' is the origin of the Hebrew word Sheen Final Mem, which we know means 'initiate', as in the phrase translated into English as "David gat him a name", meaning that David was initiated as an Israelite priest-king, essentially one who knows the secrets of working with the whole energetic system embodied within the temple. 'Hor' in the Egyptian term above is the origin of the Hebrew Hay Raysh, the omphalos, an example of which was the 'mount' where Moses received the tablets. Essentially all sacred sites, whether in Egypt, Palestine, Greece, medieval Europe, or elsewhere, are based on the same principle, in which the higher creative energies are harmonised with the dense vibrations of the three-dimensional world: in a sense they form the 'knots' in the etheric net which underlies our physical world. The priest-king directs and controls the operation of the system and, if one were to ask why our present condition on the planet is so increasingly chaotic, it is because the whole temple system is neglected and in a state of decay.

Bond and Lea say, regarding the significance of the formative number 43, raised to the power of ten, "Why this number is chosen for the purpose of symbolising the controlling factor...all that can be said is, that it controls, unites and harmonises the measures of circles and rectilinear figures in a manner no other simple number could do".[1]

As we have seen, with the developments in physics since Bond and Lea wrote and using the same principles that they established, but applied to the Hebrew text of the Old Testament, a great deal more can be said. We have seen the role of the priest-king/Pharaoh, Salmon, as intermediary in the energy flow that manifests as our planet and its creatures. We have also seen the energy links between our solar system and other parts of the galaxy and an indication of the interactions between other stellar systems.

In connection with what they call the 'First Mystery', Bond and Lea look at the power of the "powers of the Number Ten" with reference to what they call the 'Ineffable Source of All'.[2] This 'Ineffable Source' is expressed in the cabalistic tree of life (see Figure 34) by the

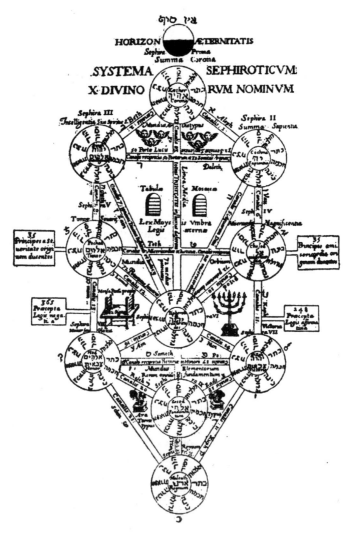

Figure 34. The Cabalistic Diagram from Kircher's "Oedipus".

Prima Sephira diagram which shows the Infinite Source in the resting state, what in Hindu philosophy is referred to as 'The Night of Brahma'. This enters the active state of manifestation, 'The Day of Brahma' by:

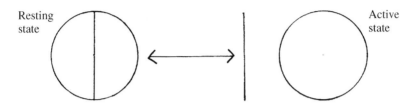

Resting state · Active state

Now we have the cosmic phallus, the creative instrument, which was contained, within the circle of infinity, emerging and becoming active. As the cabalistic tree of life shows, this emergence gives rise to the 10 sephiroth, symbolising the whole creation. Stirling[3] lists the Hebrew names for the ten Sephiroth and shows that their combined gematria add up to 2868. A circle with the circumference of 2868 has a diameter of 912 and this is the gematria of the Hebrew Brashit, Bayt Raysh Aleph Sheen Yod Tav, translated in the English as "In the beginning"[4] (Genesis 1:1). As we have just seen, this 'beginning', this initiation of an active creative phase of manifestation is precisely the cosmic phallus, represented by the straight line contained within the circle, the Prima Sephira. Furthermore, 'omphalos', the cosmic navel, written in Greek, has the gematria 911. The ithyphallic Pharaoh in Egyptian art shows the Pharaoh with his erect penis projecting from the position of his navel. This is not due to ignorance of anatomy on the part of the Egyptians, as has been suggested, but is quite deliberate, the intention being to link the navel, the site of incoming creative energies, with the phallus as the instrument by means of which these energies become manifested.

Stirling also points out that the gematria of Prometheus is 912, "who is an exact counterpart of the Hebrew Adam Kadmon, or supernal Adam, in whose person the ten steps (of the Cabala) were symbolically manifested".[5] Stirling goes on "The artificer of the gods, to whom was imputed an exquisite and marvellous skill in smith work and other crafts, was named Hephaestos, 1289, a number which is the diagonal of a square whose sides are 912". While Prometheus "taught men letters and the intellectual arts", Hephaistos "guided the hand of the artisan". In other words they both symbolise creative activity and are linked mathamatically as $1:\sqrt{2}$. This all relates to the ratio of $1:\sqrt{2}$ etc. in the

AlephBaytic cube, which expresses the essence of the creative process in relation to the cosmic scheme and the sacred text.

Prometheus was one of the four sons of the Titan Iapetus and one of his brothers was called Epimethius: Prometheus means looking forward and Epimetheus means looking back. The element 'meth' common to both names comes from the Hebrew Mem Hhayt, 'rod', for example Aaron's rod, which we know symbolises creative and destructive energy. It is the origin of the English word 'measure' and of 'metre', hence a measuring rod, an instrument determining proportion. The gematria of Mem Hhayt is 48, suggesting that it determines the harmonic basis of the Sirian system; which is founded on the 49 year orbit of Sirius B. The Hebrew Maet (Mem Hhayt) in turn comes from the Egyptian Maet, or Maat, the goddess of truth and justice. In the judgement of the dead, she was weighed against the dead, in the assessment of a person's life. Thus Epimetheus measures the past and Prometheus measures the future, in the sense of 'that which was' and 'that which is to come' in the statement "I am Alpha and Omega, that which is, that which was and that which is to come".[6] In the diagonal across the cube of letters, from Aleph at one corner, to Final Tsadde at the diagonally opposite corner, the letter Nun stands at the centre, now, the only reality.

Looking again at Prometheus and Hephaistos, Stirling says Hephaistos "only differed from Prometheus in that he guided the hand of the artisan, in contradistinction to the god, who taught men letters and the intellectual arts".[7] But we have already come across a similar pair in the Hebrew mythology: extra-biblical Hebrew myth states that Bezalel was able to use letters as creative tools, while, in the Greek myth, Prometheus "taught men letters". "[Bezalel and Oholiab] hath he filled with wisdom of the heart, to work all manner of workmanship, of the engraver, and of the cunning workman, and of the embroiderer, in blue, and in purple, in scarlet, and in fine linen, and of the weaver...".[8] Here, within the limits of the translator's understanding, is the definitive statement of the creative art.

The link between these two pairs of characters, one Hebrew and the other Greek, is remarkably born out by the gematria. We have already seen that the name Bezalel in Hebrew has the gematria of 153 and, reducing this by 1, as allowed by the law of Colel, to make it 152, then $6 \times 152 = 912$, which is the gematria of Prometheus. We saw that the gematria of Bezalel, one hundred, fifty and three, is a hologram for the AlephBaytic cube, locating its centre and two corners (Figure 7). Here the diagonals linking the centre to each corner have a ratio of $\sqrt{3}:1$, when the sides of the eight cubic modules making up the large cube are equal to 1. In the same way, the ratio of the gematria of Prometheus, 912, to that of Hephaistos, 1289, is $1 : \sqrt{2}$, that of one side of a module to the diagonal of its face.

The gematria of Aholiab, Aleph Hay Lammed Yod AlephBayt, the craftsman partner of Bezalel, is 49, while that of the Hebrew Mayt (rod) is 48, so that he embodies the sacred measures expressed in his work. These all relate to each other as the roots of numbers, $1 : \sqrt{3}$ being the ratio of feet to Royal Cubits (1:1.72) foot to megalithic yard (1:2.72) and so on. As we saw in Figure 11, these geometric proportions of the physical creation are synthesised in the equilateral triangle, in which the ratio of its half base to its height is $1 : \sqrt{3}$ and that of its height to the length of its sides is 8:9, that of the major whole tone in music. The whole creation and all properly designed works of man express this synthesis.

Remarkable though it may be, the reader may not be surprised to discover that there is a link between Bond and Lea's work on the gematria of the Greek text of the New Testament and Greek mythology at a fundamental level. We have already seen evidence of this connection in the gematria of the Hebrew Bezalel and Aholiab and the Greek Prometheus and Hephaistos, each pair being involved with the creative process. Furthermore, the links with Prometheus go to the heart of Bond and Lea's thesis. Regarding "the second cube difference, namely 19 [in the Metacubes], [this] is 27 minus 8. Just as 37, the third cubes difference, is the basic number of the Christos series of names, so is 19 that of the names and titles of the Virgin Mary".[9]

If we then divide 912 by 2, we get 456, the gematria of the Greek 'meter', mother, the number of visible points, 19, multiplied by 24. Figure 25 shows stages in the development of the Cosmic Scheme and in 25(c) we have the first appearance of a straight line, AB. In the Prima Sephira this is the line contained within the circle, which emerges to initiate the creative process, the omphalos, or Omphallus, universal phallus, or instrument of creation. The gematria of omphalos is 911 and the gematria of Prometheus is 912, giving the link with the creative process in Greek mythology through Prometheus and Hephaistos and with the same in Hebrew through Bezalel and Aholiab.

Figure 24(e) shows the circle, together with its contained line AB and the rectangle JKLM, which forms the basis of the musical proportions. In (f) the musical proportions are completed within JKLM and the diagonals JL and MK form the base note in the octave whose proportions are expressed geometrically within JKLM. But JK and LM are, like AB, diagonals of the containing circle with centre 0, whose length is 912, the gematria of Prometheus. Thus 'Prometheus' embodies the whole geometric and musical basis of the physical world, confirming his role as "mediator between heaven and earth".[10] The octave is completed by JM (or KL) and this is equal to AB/2, so that, if AB = 912, then JM = 912/2 = 456, mother ('meter' in Greek). A similar idea is expressed in Figure 29, where the mother/wife has a height equal to 2/7ths of the height of the Pharaoh, the length of the Covered Temple and the Outer Court on the temple plan and the height of the new-born in proportion to the adult Pharaoh. Here we have the microcosm, the temple and the man (and woman) expressed, together with the macro-cosm, embodied in the deity, in this case Prometheus.

One crucial aspect of Bond and Lea's second cube, the Cube of the Mother, is its 19 visible points, that aspect of the whole energy body made up of the 27 points (and hence the 27 letters of the AlephBayt), that these 19 constitute the physical expression of the underlying creative energy. In terms of the living world, plants, animals and bacteria, in spite of their immense variety, they are all made up of proteins and, although there are a large number of these, they are all made up of just 20 different amino acids (in animals. There are 22 altogther, two occuring only in plants and bacteria). "The spatial structure of proteins (and therefore of amino acids) requires – in contrast to normal chemical compounds – that they be described with the terms 'left' and 'right': analogous to the left and right hand". When light is passed through proteins in a spectro-meter it is turned either to the left, or to the right, according to the protein being examined. "One thing about these amino acids I found particularly intriguing. They are made up of 19 left-oriented amino acids [and] one amino acid that has no optical centre and that therefore can be said to have both a left and right orientation".[11] Therefore, the 19 points in the visible faces of the $2 \times 2 \times 2$ Cube of the Mother correspond to the 19 left-oriented amino acids and the twentieth one, which has both left and right orientation is located at the centre of the cube, the location of the Hebrew letter Nun, "that which is" between "that which was and that which is to come"[12] and therefore is facing both ways. And of course, "that which was" is Epimetheus and "that which is to come" is Prometheus.

Looking again at Figure 24(e) and (f), we know that the circle with centre 0 and diameter AB represents 'Prometheus'. Figure 35 shows the Cosmic Scheme in two dimensions, so that the AlephBaytic cube appears as the hexagon NOPQRST. This hexagon contains the 19 points in the cube when viewed from this position, with the Hebrew Final Tsadde at the centre. These are also the locations of the 19 left-rotating amino acids. The circle AB, 'Prometheus', contains this hexagon and the creative energy embodied by the 'god' is manifested

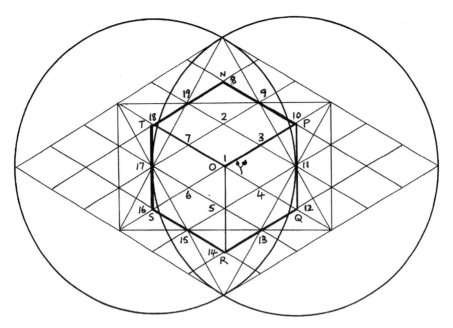

Figure 35. The AlephBaytic cube and the nineteen left-rotating amino acids. The cube in two dimensions, forming the hexagon NPQRST.

physically as these amino acids synthesised into proteins, as the bodies of living organisms.

Plichta states that of the 81 stable elements in the periodic table, "57 elements, ie 3 × 19 have divisible atomic numbers and the remaining 19 have atomic numbers which are prime numbers".[13] The reappearance of the number 19 could be dismissed as mere coincidence: after all what connection is there between amino acids and chemical elements? The obvious answer is that amino acids, like any chemical compounds, are composed of elements. If we rotate the cube of letters through 180 degrees, we now have the letter Aleph at the centre and again there are 19 of the total 27 points and their corresponding Hebrew letters visible (see Figure 36). This shows Plichta's group of 19 elements whose atomic numbers are also prime numbers arranged in the positions of the 19 visible points when viewed from this side. This group of 19 can be further divided into two groups: one consisting of 7 points, the central one and the 6 forming the small hexagon and the remaining 12 in the large hexagon around the edge. It is only the inner 7 positions that cannot be seen from the other side; the outer 12 can be seen from both sides.

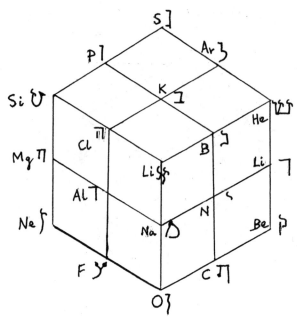

Figure 36. Plichta's first group of 19 elements and the AlephBaytic cube. The cube is reversed, with Aleph replacing Final Tsadde at the centre. This and the six elements in the inner cube all have atomic numbers which are prime numbers and occur in Plichta's first ring of numbers up to 24.

The 7 elements placed at the centre and in the inner hexagon are distinguished from the remaining 12 in that they are all in Plichta's first ring of 24, being all the prime numbers in this ring (see Figure 14).

So far we have placed 19 elements, but there is a twentieth which, like the other 19, has an atomic number that can only be divided by 1 and that is hydrogen, whose atomic number is 1 itself. "Of all the elements in the periodic system, the first element – hydrogen, which has the atomic number 1 – is the maverick of the herd and was for that reason the subject of considerable dispute among chemists" and there is no logical place for it in the periodic table. "Hydrogen is (on the other hand) the basic building-block of matter. Just as all numbers can in the end be derived from the number 1, all elements on the earth were created in a flash in an exploding star from the first element, hydrogen".[14] This gives an astonishing insight into the origins of matter.

So, it is appropriate that hydrogen should be the eighth element in the central group and the twentieth in the group of 19 + 1 on this side of the cube. But where is a place for it? All the points are already filled.

However, there is a place which perfectly suits its unique characteristics among all the 81 stable elements. This is at the centre of the cube, the sun at the centre of the constellation of elements, the source from which they are all derived, "and in the midst of the candlesticks one like unto a son (Sun) of man".[15] As we already know, this central point in the Menorah (six-branched candlestick) is also the central point of the cube.

12

THE HOLY CITY CRYSTALS

"... and behold, a door opened in heaven, and the first voice which I heard, a voice as of a trumpet speaking with me and saying, Come up hither, and I will show thee the things which must come to pass hereafter. Straightway I was in the Spirit: and behold there was a throne set in heaven, and one sitting upon the throne. And he that sat was to look upon like a jasper stone and a sardius; and there was a rainbow around about the throne, like an emerald to look upon. And around about the throne were four and twenty thrones: and upon the thrones I saw four and twenty elders sitting, arrayed in white garments, and upon their heads crowns of gold. And out of the throne proceeded lightnings and voices and thunders. And there were seven lamps of fire burning before the throne, which are the seven spirits of God. And before the throne, as it were a glassy sea like unto crystal; and in the midst of the throne, four living creatures full of eyes, before and behind. And the first creature was like a lion, and the second creature like a calf, and the third creature had the face as of a man, and the fourth creature was like a flying eagle".[1]

This magisterial description of the processes underlying creation ends with a reference to Ezekiel's four 'creatures' or 'faces' and Ezekiel 1:13 refers to a fire "down among the living creatures and out of the fire went forth lightning",[2] which is also referred to in this passage from Revelation as 'lightnings' etc. emanating from the throne. Revelation refers to "a rainbow round about the throne" and Ezekeil 1:28 refers to a throne with "the appearance of a bow that is in the cloud in the day of rain".[3]

The passage from Revelation begins with "... a door opened in heaven" and 'the door' in Greek is 'e lyra', whose gematria is 518 which is equal to 37 × 14. In Greek 'heaven' is 'ouranos', whose gematria is 891, which Bond and Lea state is 11 times the square of nine and they show a circle whose diameter is 284, the gematria of 'Theos', God and

$\pi \times 284 = 891$. Bond and Lea show this circle enclosed by a square and its perimeter is 1136, which is the gematria of 'mesouranos', the mid-heaven.[4] A key word in this passage from Revelation is 'trumpet', whose voice is heard, giving impetus to the creative process. The Hebrew word for 'trumpet' is Sheen Phay Raish, sh-f-r, the origin of our word cipher, a secret language and it is precisely this secret language, that of creation, that the voice of the trumpet is speaking. Ezekiel refers to the 'terrible crystal' above the four creatures and he describes "the likeness of a throne, as the appearance of a sapphire stone"[5] and Revelation states that "he that sat (upon the throne was) to look upon like a jasper stone and a sardius", i.e. crystalline. But 'sapphire' in Hebrew is Sammekh Phay Yod Raish, phonetically almost identical to sheen Phay Raish, trumpet. Hence this "secret language" synthesises the musical and crystalline basis of the creative process, with terms such as 'jasper' and 'sardius' indicating the general crystalline basis of the process, with reference to its physical expression and the crystalline basis of matter. Figure 37 shows the crystalline structure of chrysolite, the seventh of the twelve crystals in St.

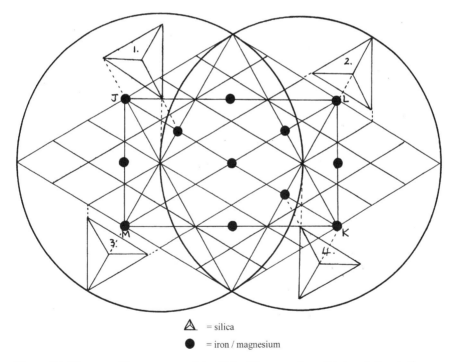

$\triangle$ = silica

● = iron / magnesium

Figure 37. The crystalline structure of the Holy City gem chrysolite in relation to the Cosmic Scheme. The silica tetrahedra link to the rectangle while the intersecting circles and the metal atoms relate to the musical proportions.

John's foundations of the new Jerusalem,[6] in the context of the Cosmic Scheme. It consists of tetrahedra of silica, which appear as equilateral triangles in two dimensions and atoms of either iron or magnesium, shown as small circles. The figure shows how the component atoms fit into the geometry. The sides of the tetrahedra of silica are equal to JM/2, resonating to a note one octave above that of JM. The distance between the metalic atoms is also equal to JM/2. Nearly all the Holy City jewels are silicates, containing the same tetrahedral as chrysolite, the exception being sapphire.

Why are all the Holy City jewels except sapphire silicates? This fact suggests the importance of silica and of the silica tetrahedra (see Figure 39). Each of the four faces of the tetrahedral is an equilateral triangle and we know that the ratio of the length of each side in this triangle to its height is 9:8, the ratio of the major wholetone in music and we know that the sides of the faces of these tetrahedra are equal to JM/2. Therefore, if for example, JM = 18, then the sides of the tetrahedra will be 9 and their height (AO in Figure 11) will be 8. Thus, each tetrahedron of silica will vibrate harmonically in response to any energy input, and in harmony with the rest of the Cosmic Scheme, whose proportions are the same. Of course, in terms of the human auditory range, the scale of the instruments producing the sound, open pipes etc., is very large compared to that at the atomic level of the crystal structure and any sound will be at the level of very high frequencies, at the microwave level, but it is the proportions that are important.

On the scale of the sacred building, temple etc., the fabric of the building is essentially the stone, whose crystalline structure acts as a harmonic resonator in response to the incoming creative energies and those evoked in the breastplate etc. and the body of the High Priest. "And the house, when it was building, was built of stone made ready at the quarry: and there was neither hammer, nor axe, nor any tool of iron heard in the house when it was building".[7] This passage hints at the sensitivity of the system, exemplified here by the Salmon's temple and there is a specific reason for this, which concerns the harmonic resonance based on the crystalline structure of the stone from which the temple is built. A characteristic of crystals, such as quartz, which are composed of silica, is that pressure applied to the crystal causes it to emit electricity, a piezo-electric effect. This is due to distortion caused by the pressure and any such distortion will change the harmonic characteristics of the crystals, and hence of the whole structure, so that it will no longer work in a harmonious way. By using bronze or wooden tools any distortion in the quarried stone could be avoided.

The gematria of the Hebrew text of 1 Kings 6:7 confirms that it is concerned with the harmonic properties of the stone: in the phrase "when it was building", in the Hebrew text, 'building' has the gematria of 465, the gematria of the Greek 'ē mētēr', the Mother and the gematria of 'meter' is 456. As we know, if AB in the Cosmic Scheme is equal to 912, the gematria of Prometheus, then JM, which is equal to AB/2, is 456. Here we have the suggestion of the Mother in relation to the temple plan, JKLM in the Cosmic Scheme, in the same way as we saw at Luxor, in relation to the Pharaoh (Figure 29). At Chartres cathedral, on the south side of the choir, is the Belle Verrière window with the figure of the Mother and Child (Figure 38). This fits into the plan of the cathedral when scaled up, in the same way as the figure of the

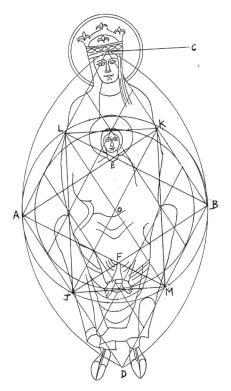

Figure 38. The Child in the Mother's womb in La Belle Verrière. The geometry of the Cosmic Scheme superimposed on the stained glass picture of the Mother and Child at Chartres cathedral. The base of the Mother's spine is at F, with Her knees drawn up to AOB, so that her navel and that of the Child are at the centre O. In an emerald crystal, beryllium atoms are located at J, K, L, M and 0 and there are aluminium atoms at E and F.

Pharaoh at Luxor. Her head even has a slight tilt, corresponding to the slight tilt towards the north of the apse of the cathedral.

Then, in the Hebrew text of "the house, when it was building", Vav Hay Bayt Yod Tav Bayt Hay Bayt Nun Tav Vav, we have the gematria 888 ($= 37 \times 24$), where, as Bond and Lea point out, $19:37::456:888$,[8] in which 19 is the number of visible points on the Cube of Two, 37 is the number visible on the Cube of Four, $19 \times 24 = 456$, "the number of visible points, each counted as 24" and $37 \times 24 = 888$, the number of visible points on the Cube of Four, each counted as 24. These two numbers, 456 and 888, represent the manifestation of Mother and Son, as in the stained glass of the Belle Verrière window at Chartres. This is shown in Figure 40, contained in part of the geometry of the Cosmic Scheme.

Verse 7 of 1 Kings 6 goes on "the house . . . was built of stone" and the gematria of 'stone' in the Hebrew is $703 = 37 \times 19$, a reference to the visible points of the two cubes, confirming the link with Mother and Son.

All this brings out the significance of Jesus' statement "Destroy this temple, and in three days I will raise it up . . . but he spake of the temple of his body".[9] In fact he was speaking of both, as illustrated by the Pharaoh and the temple plan at Luxor and of the Mother and Child and the plan at Chartres.

We saw that the Hebrew words for 'trumpet' and 'sapphire' are almost identical, sh-ph-r and s-phir respectively, and the link between the creative (or destructive) sound and its resonance with the atomic structures of specific crystals, such as the silica tetrahedra. But why, out of the twelve Holy City jewels, are eleven of them silicates, with a main component of their structure consisting of silica tetrahedra, while the twelfth, sapphire, is composed of aluminium oxide. This difference suggests that there is some property of sapphire and perhaps of the corundum group of crystals in general (including ruby), which is distinctive from those of the other eleven crystals and which is necessary for the functioning of the creative system. Ezekiel gives a hint as to what this property may be: "The appearance of the wheels and their work was like unto the colour of a beryl".[10] Beryl, like sapphire, is an aluminium oxide. It only differs from emerald in that in the latter 0.5% of the aluminium is replaced by chromium, but this impurity gives the emerald a brilliant green colour, when compared with the relatively dull green of beryl.

This 'impurity' brings us to the property of aluminium silicates, such as emerald and ruby, which is that they can behave as lasers. When a ruby crystal is exposed to a beam of red light, electrons in the chromium atoms are shifted into an orbit one further out from the nucleus. Then, when the beam of light is shut off, the electrons return to their normal orbits and a beam of coherent light (i.e. of one wavelength) is emitted. This gives a beam of intense energy concentrated into a very small area.

"And over the head of the living creature there was the likeness of a firmament, like the colour of the terrible crystal...".[11] Laser action gives an indication of this immense power present in the jewel. In the Hebrew text the word translated as 'colour' is Bayt Ayn Yod Final Nun, whose gematria is 800, the eighth step in the crane dance, leading to a higher dimension. It is also the gematria of the Greek 'choinix', a measure, and here we have the suggestion of a dance as "treading a measure".

In the Hebrew of "the terrible crystal", 'crystal' is Nun Tayt Vav Yod, whose gematria is 75 and the root of the Hebrew word translated as 'time' is 74. As we know, this relates to the phrase in Daniel 12:7, "time, times and half a time", indicating the two octaves D (37 Hz), D (74 Hz) and d (148 Hz). In the Cosmic Scheme these correspond to AB, JM and the sides of the quartz tetrahedra in the chrysolite crystal, the frequency ratios of 1:2:4.

Written in Greek we have Prometheus = 912, JK in the Cosmic Scheme, while JM = 456, 912/2. In Figure 40, this is reversed, with the Child being contained within a rhombus whose length is half that containing the Mother. In this remarkable work of stained glass the significance of the geometry and crystallography is determined by the fact that the Mother is squatting, so that the base of her spine lies between the Child's calves and their navels are both at the centre 0. Then, if the larger circle with centre 0 is the womb, containing the Child, the Child is indeed linked by its navel to the Mother, "How beautiful are thy feet in sandals O prince's daughter! The joints of thy thighs are like jewels...".[12] The artist has emphasised the sandals by tilting the Mother's feet forward and, because she is squatting, the upper joints of the thigh bones, between the thighs and pelvis, are at the level JM and the lower joints, the knees, are on the line AOB. In an emerald crystal, J, M and O are the positions of beryllium atoms in a beryl or emerald crystal and an aluminium atom is located at F (at the base of the mother's spine), also at E. "Thy navel is like a round goblet, wherein no mingled wine is wanting".[13] If one imagines one is looking down into, say, a brandy glass, from vertically above, with the stem at 0, then the rim of the glass forms the inner circle and the belly of the glass is the outer circle. The "mingled wine" is the mother's blood flowing through the umbilical cord and Child's navel together with the latter's blood. As we saw, because the Mother is crouching, her navel and that of the child are in line at O, emphasising the 'mingling'. The central beryllium atom is located at this point, underlining the crystallographic basis of the whole picture.

The outer of the two circles centred at 0 is the womb and the inner one is the amnion. The latter contains the body of the Child, except for his feet, indicating that the waters have broken and the birth has begun. Being feet first, it is a breech birth, suggesting the immense challenges in the lifetime to come.

We now come to the crucial issue which derives from the difference between the eleven silicate minerals which make up all but one of the Holy City jewels and the twelfth, the beryl, or emerald. This latter belongs to the corundum group, all of which are aluminium oxides and it is the aluminium in the jewel that gives the distinctive difference between the eleven silicates and this odd-one-out. In the beryl/emerald, the aluminium atoms are located at E and F in the Cosmic Scheme. As we saw, the difference between beryl and emerald is that, in the latter, 0.5% of the aluminium is replaced by chromium and this 'impurity' is responsible for the brilliant green colour of emerald, as compared to the relatively dull colour of beryl.

We also know that, in the case of ruby, another gem in the group of aluminium oxides, the same replacement of 0.5% of the aluminium by chromium gives the possibility of laser action when such a jewel is exposed to red light. This energy input causes electrons in the chromium atoms to move into an orbit one step further out from the nucleus. Then when the red light entering the crystal is cut off, the electrons all return to their original orbits and this releases a pulse of coherent light, i.e. of one wavelength. Such pure light was hitherto unknown and is a result of what is called laser action. With the laser phenomenon in mind, we can look again at Bond and Lea's investigation of the mystical aspects of light and the gematria associated with it. They show seven rays associated with the "New Creation symbolised by the Cube", but they point out that "the reputed seven colours of the spectrum are really Three... the Red, the Green and the Violet-blue". The authors show in the Cube of Light, that the three rays have lengths that relate to each other as 1, $\sqrt{2}$ and $\sqrt{3}$. Then, referring to the wavelengths of light, they show that red, green and violet light relate to each other in the same way, so that if the wavelength of green is taken as equal to 1, then $1 \times \sqrt{2}$ gives a red colour near the lower end of the visible spectrum and $1/\sqrt{3}$ gives the wavelength of light at the upper end of the spectrum, a colour "of the most intense deep blue".[14] Then, with reference to the "three kinds of light in the Lord's endyma [robes]" described in the Pistis Sophia and the relevant gematria, they link these with the three colours, "if it be true that the data of the colour scale – which are derived from molecular motions – are indeed founded upon harmonics whose source is not, as in the case of sound and other physical measure, based upon the interaction of forces having whole-number proportions, but upon those mysterious entities, the Roots of Two and Three, then we are face to face with a condition pointing to a genesis of motion in a region of space unknown to us, and wherein the dynamic laws operate in a relation quite unfamiliar".[15]

When Bond and Lea wrote this, Newtonian physics was beginning to crumble in the face of the development of quantum mechanics. Order, certainty, the feeling that there was little further to be discovered had been replaced, first by Einstein and then by the quantum mechanics, by a completely new view of the basis of the physical creation, by doubt and apparent contradiction. There is nothing to suggest that our authors were aware of this, which makes their insights all the more remarkable. Perhaps their reference to "a genesis of motion in a region of space unknown to us" may be taken to refer to the discoveries being made even as they wrote. Certainly the discovery of the phenomenon of laser action, a practical outcome of quantum mechanics, came after our authors had moved to a higher plane of existence, but their work on the three rays can surely be regarded as prophetic.

Returning to the matter of crystals and lasers, we can equate Bond and Lea's red, green and blue rays with three varieties of corundum, or aluminium oxide: ruby, emerald and sapphire, in which 0.5% of the aluminium is replaced by chromium, in which the laser action can be initiated. In the Cosmic Scheme we saw that the sides of the tetrahedra of silica had a length equal to JM/2. If we measure the diameter of the Child's halo, we find that this is also equal to JM/2 and this suggests that, like the silica tetrahedra, the halo may play a part in the resonance of the crystal and, since the halo consists of light, the resonance may occur within the light spectrum. Furthermore, we know that E is a major energy centre in the Cosmic Scheme and this is the location of an aluminium atom in the ruby crystal. Then, if the aluminium atom is actually centred at P in Figure 40, the centre of the Child's forehead, then E may indicate the position of an electron in orbit around P, the orbital path being indicated by the outline of the halo. The high energy associated with E in the Scheme suggests that this is the orbit into which the electron has been displaced after the input of red light, before returning to its stable orbit, with the emission of a pulse of coherent light. The Greek 'halos', meaning the disc of the Sun or Moon, is the origin of our word halo and this confirms the link with an intense energy source. The gematria of 'halos' is 1031 and $1030/2 = 515$, the gematria of the Greek word 'parthenos', 'virgin' and here we have, in the stained glass at Chartres, the Virgin Mother. Furthermore,

'parthenos' (virgin) $= 515$

'e katabole aletheias' $= 704$, EF in the Cosmic Scheme
(the true conception)

'o logos ek patros' $(515 + 704) = 1219$, 'ichthys' (fish)
(the word out of the Father[16]).

And $704 = $ EF, while $1219 = $ AB in the Cosmic Scheme. All this links the medieval stained glass picture to Bond and Lea's Cabala of the Fish and the Cosmic Scheme.

As we saw, 'parthenos' combined with 'o aner' (the man), $515 + 229 = 744$, the gematria of 'ē Mētēr Semelē', the Mother Semele, written in Greek and she is "spouse of Zeus, who gives birth to Dionysos"[17] so that the gematria reveal the fact that the Judaeo-Christian and Greek myths concern the same events.

13

AGNI AND JESUS

Figure 39 shows Ernest McClain's view of the Vedic myth concerning the birth of the Son.[1] This is in the form of a tone mandala, with the tonic, the note D, at the top. The rising notes are shown on the left and their reciprocals, the falling notes, are on the right-hand side of the mandala. There is a slight discrepancy between each pair of notes and this is cumulative, so that a gap opens up at the bottom of the mandala, between G and A. The mandala represents the "womb of Usas, daughter of the Sun", in the Ṛg Veda.[2]

To the rationalist mind this discrepancy between the rising notes and their reciprocals, "too small for use as a melodic interval, so nearly subliminal under most circumstances as to invite our glossing over it", is a cause of considerable unease and is an example of a much more general anxiety among scientists in general and particle physicists in particular: that the further they go in their investigation of quantum mechanics, the more difficult it becomes to maintain a rationalist position. The problem may be resolved by the acceptance and fundamental importance of the irrational and, by implication, of the reality of levels of existence beyond the perception of our physical senses, McClain solves the particular discrepancy between A and G by making them equal to $\sqrt{2}$, which, of course, represents an irrational value.

Taking McClain's tonic (or base note) of D (74 Hz), then $74 \times 2 = 104$ Hz, just halfway between G (99 Hz) and A (110 Hz), while bearing in mind that $\sqrt{2}$, being an irrational value, cannot be measured exactly. Therefore we must launch ourselves off the apparent safety of the rational world, into the dangerous, but creative world of the irrational. It is only then that our 'Agni', our awareness of our spiritual nature, can be born. As we have seen, Bond and Lea's argument is based on the roots of numbers and their $2 \times 2 \times 2$ cube, our AlephBaytic

111

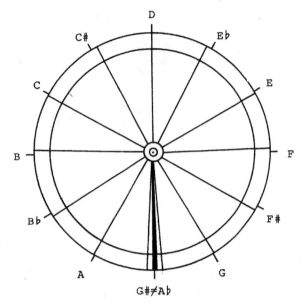

Figure 39. The musical symbolism and the Vedic myth of the birth of Agni. The discrepancy between rising and falling notes of the tone mandala reaches a point between the notes A and G where it cannot be evaded, between A flat and G sharp. In Vedic myth, this is the vagina of Usas. Mathematically it corresponds to 2, an irrational value which cannot be measured exactly.

cube, so foursquare and rational in its outward appearance, has proportions that are entirely based on the roots of 2 and 3 etc.

"It is this locus", at the point of the discrepancy between the notes A and G, "that Agni is born ... god of fire". Figure 40 shows McClain's tone mandala of the birth of Agni drawn on the Mother's womb in Figure 40. The way in which the Gothic, Christian stained glass fits with McClain's representation of the Vedic myth concerning Agni's birth is surely astonishing. We already know that the Mother's waters have broken, the Child's feet having begun to emerge from the amnion and the gematria of 'amnion' in Greek is 221/while that of 'thalassa' (sea), is 442, which is equal to 221 × 2. The amnion recreates within the Mother's womb the environment from which our remote ancestors evolved.

The intervals marked by the notes of the tone mandala fit perfectly with the diamond lattice on which the crystal structure and the musical proportions developed within the rectangle JKLM are based. Most remarkably of all, the Child's feet mark the tonal discrepancy between the ascending and descending scales, the point at which Agni emerges

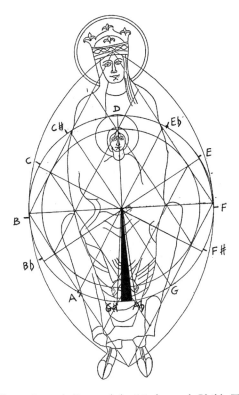

Figure 40. The Vedic music symbolism and the Mother and Child. The outer circle with centre O is now the womb of Usas, the mother of Agni, the Fire God. The tonal discrepancy between A flat and G sharp cannot be evaded. It is at this point of tension that Agni is born.

from the womb. We have already seen the way in which the apparent musical discrepancy, viewed rationally, between A and G at this point on the tone mandala, is resolved by introducing the irrational value $\sqrt{2}$, i.e. by raising consciousness to a higher level. This shift of consciousness sets the tone for the incarnation whose commencement is shown in the picture, that of the Vedic Agni and the Piscean Avatar Jesus.

The writer of the Apocalypse refers back[3] to Ezekiel's four creatures[4] and the latter confirms that we are dealing with crystalline structure and specifically with 'beryl': "The appearance of the wheels and their work was like unto the colour of beryl" and the reference to 'their work' suggests their movement in orbit around the nucleus of the atoms, the 'wheels' being the orbits. The gematria of 'wheels' in Hebrew is Vav Yod Ayn Sheen Hay, whose gematria is 1001 and 'warp', 'woof' (in "either warp or woof"[5]) has the gematria 1004, the 'warp and woof' of the crystal being the lattice within which the atoms of aluminium, beryllium, chromium etc. are placed. Then we have "before the throne, as it were a glassy sea, like unto a crystal".[6] Here 'throne' is used to suggest the foundation or basis of creation, echoing the role of the fundamental forces (the four 'creatures') and both 'thronos' and 'valine', 'throne' and 'glassy', have the gematria of 499, indicating the crystalline structure of all matter. Then, as we saw, the gematria of 'thalassa' (sea) is 442 and that of 'amnion', the foetal sea, is 221 (= 442/2), confirming the picture of Mother and Child as an illustration of the creative process.

The word 'wheels' brings us to another aspect of the Mother and Child at Chartres. We have already seen the links between this medieval Christian picture and the Vedic myth concerning the birth of Agni and its musical significance. In the Vedic system the physical body is said to be linked to its counterparts at higher energy levels through a series of seven vortices, named chakras, or 'wheels'. These are situated between the base of the spine and the crown of the head. The health of the body is dependent on the free and harmonious flow of energy through the chakras. Written in Greek as 'xakra', the gematria is 722 and $720 = 30 \times 24$, the gematria of 'Mother of Truth' and 'Topos', 'the abode of Deity'. In the Chartres stained glass we have profound truths expressed in the figure of the Mother.

The Sanskrit word 'chakra' is the origin of our word 'chariot' and the Hebrew word for chariot is merkabah, whose root is Mem Raish Kaf, whose gematria is 259, which is equal to 37×7, the gematria of the Greek word 'basileia', meaning 'kingdom'. In Vedic symbolism Indra's chariot wheel is the tone mandala, shown in Figure 42. Here, as we have seen, Indra-Agni is born in the segment of the mandala between the notes A and G. Opposite this segment is the note D, the tonic, or base note, of the octave and in Vedic myth this is the linchpin of Indra's chariot wheel. We also know that the note D, two octaves below middle C, is the base note of the two octave series D_1, D, d, derived from the phrase "Time, times and half a time",[7] in which D_1 is 37 Hz, corresponding to Bond and Lea's gematric series based on multiples of 37 and in which the root of the Hebrew word for 'time' is Ayn Dallet, whose gematria is 74 ($= 37 \times 2$).

There are seven chakras and these are located along the central nervous system (spinal cord and brain). Each chakra is associated with an endocrine gland, which acts as an intermediary between the higher energies entering through the chakras and the physical body. In Figures 40 and 42 the Mother's chakras extend from a point midway between J and M, which is the base of her spine and the centre of her crown at

C, the location of her crown chakra, the position of her base chakra being due to the fact that she is squatting. This squatting posture brings her third chakra into line with the Child's third chakra at 0 and hence into line with the geometry; crystallography and musical proportions, revealing that all these underlie the proportions of the human body. 0 is at the centre of the two rhombuses, one containing the Child and one the Mother; it is at the intersection of the two diagonals, JK and LM, which establish the tonic, or base note; for the musical proportions underlying the picture and it is the position of the central beryllium atom in the beryl/emerald crystal.

In corundum crystals, such as ruby and sapphire, aluminium atoms are located at the base of the Mother's spine, the position of her first chakra and at the Child's neck, the location of his fifth chakra.

Figure 41 shows an enlargement of the upper part of the Chartres stained glass. The Child's fifth, sixth and seventh chakras are shown: the sixth is at the centre of the circle which indicates the Child's halo

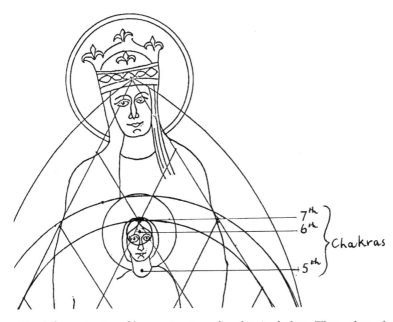

Figure 41. A demonstration of laser action in medieval stained glass. The nucleus of an aluminium atom is assumed to be at the centre of the Son's forehead, at the centre of his halo and a second smaller circle is drawn inside it. These are taken to represent two electron shells within the aluminium atom. Input of light of a given frequency causes electrons to move from the inner to the outer shell. When the input ceases, the electrons return to the inner orbit and a pulse of coherent light is emitted.

115

and a second, smaller, circle is shown with the same centre and with its circumference passing through his crown chakra, the position of an aluminium atom in ruby etc. If we assume that this is a site where a chromium atom has replaced the aluminium, then the input of greenish-yellow light will initiate laser action: assuming that the smaller circle represents the orbital path of an electron in the atom before the input, then the larger circle represents the path taken up by the electron at the moment of input and when this ceases the electron returns to the former path. This is accompanied by the emission of coherent light, the laser beam. The resting state marked by the small circle is tangent to JM, whose length corresponds to the tonic of the second octave (JK and LM corresponding to that of the octave below). The circumference of this circle, the inner orbit, is equal to the distance KL/6, suggesting a harmonic relationship between the orbiting electron and that of the harmonic basis of the system as a whole. The circumference of the outer orbit around the Child's sixth chakra is tangential to the larger of the two circles centred at 0, representing the Mother's womb, and the length of this outer orbital path is equal to the distance KL/2, which is the length of the sides of the silica tetrahedra in the crystals of chrysolite, which form part of the Cosmic Scheme. So, if the diagonals JK and LM represent the base note of the musical aspect of the Scheme, and this is the note D (37 Hz), then we have the following series underlying the system:

Geometry, Music and Crystallography

D_1 (37 Hz)	D (74 Hz)	d (148 Hertz
JK/LM	JM/KL	Sides of the silica tetrahedra and outer orbit of electron

The difference between the inner and outer orbits of the electron in the chromium atom centred at the Child's sixth chakra is also the difference between the two circles with centre 0 in Figure 40, the womb and the amnion. All this can be transposed up to galactic levels and beyond, the frequencies changing, but the harmonic proportions remaining constant.

We know that, in the above series, 37 is the 'base note' of Bond and Lea's gematric series and that 74 is the gematria of the Hebrew Ayn Dallet, the root of the Hebrew word for 'time' and our measurement of time is based on the orbital motion of electrons in crystals. This links in with our musical series, illustrated in Figure 41, which has the same electronic basis. "And behold, there was a throne set in heaven, and one sitting upon the throne; and he that sat was to look upon like a jasper stone".[8] In the Cosmic Scheme the throne is at 0, which is also the centre of Figure 40, so that "the one like unto a jasper stone" is at 0. In the Greek text 'stone' is 'lithō', whose gematria is 849.

Here Bond and Lea discuss the "Cabala of the Cosmos": "The formative principle expressed by the mathematical powers One, Root Two and Root Three, are assumed as the Aeons whose operation has been invoked to bring into manifestation the visible Universe".[9] In the AlephBaytic Cube these Aeons are expressed as the length of one side (One), the diagonal of that side ($\sqrt{2}$) and the internal diagonal of the Cube, for example, from Aleph to Final Tsadde ($\sqrt{3}$). In this context of the Letter Cube, we see the literal operation of the Aeons in "bringing into manifestation the visible Universe".

Our authors take as the first Aeon, One, the Greek word 'kosmos', whose gematria is 600. The second Aeon is the $\sqrt{2} \times 600$, "848 or 849 and the Greek term 'megas kosmos', the macrocosm, is 848 and the gematria of the Greek 'lithō' (stone), in the phrase "like unto a jasper stone", is 849, referring to the central point 0 in the Cosmic Scheme. Whereas the macrocosm suggests the infinitely large, the point at the centre indicates the infinitely small. These are combined in Figure 25(a), where we have the first stage in the development of the Scheme shown as a circle with its central point. It is from these two apparent opposites, the infinitely large and the infinitely small, that the three-dimensional world grows, as demonstrated in Figure 25.

Bond and Lea's third Aeon is $600 \times \sqrt{3}$, which is equal to 1040, the gematria of 'micros kosmos' and 1041 is the gematria of 'Sōma', the "juice of the Moon".[10] Blavatsky goes on to associate 'Sōma' with the Hermaphrodite Conception and it is the result of this Conception which is illustrated in the picture of the Mother and Child at Chartres.[11] As we know, Bond and Lea refer to the Theotokos, the union of two principles, whose gematria is 744

$$\text{'parthenos' (virgin)} = 515$$

$$+ \quad \text{('o aner' the man)} = 229$$

$$= 774$$

where 'Sōma' is the lunar or feminine aspect, Bond and Lea's third Aeon. Figure 25(a) is thus an illustration of these two principles, the central point and the circle. This figure shows the stages resulting from this union, leading up to the completion of the Cosmic Scheme, which underlies the whole physical creation.

Bond and Lea continue, this union of two principles "recalls the 'ē hermathēnē parthenos' (gematria = 744) of the older Greeks. She appears to correspond to 'ē mētēr Semelē' (= 744), the spouse of Zeus, who gives birth to Dionysos, whose name is a clever anagram of 'nous dios' – the Mind of Zeus". Clearly Semele represents the lunar aspect and Zeus the solar. Referring to the three Aeons, Bond and Lea state that "Kosmos is the pattern as conceived in the Mind of God",[12] confirming the correspondence with the Greek myth of the birth of Dionysos.

The Third Aeon, 'mikros kosmos', has the gematria 1040 and this is also the gematria of the Greek word 'chores', 'a round dance'. In Figure 42 this 'round dance' appears as the tone mandala, whose base note D lies at the intersection of the Child's halo with the circle of the Mother's womb and whose conflict between G sharp and A flat is resolved by introducing $\sqrt{2}$, leading to the birth of Agni. The notes dance around the circle of the womb/mandala, making the harmonies which underlie the creation.

The circle of the womb/mandala also contains the hexagon ALKBMJ which, seen in three dimensions, makes Bond and Lea's Cube of Four, with two of its corners in line at the centre 0. Considering the latter, its sides, LK, KB etc. make the first Aeon, 600 ('kosmos'); the diagonals of its sides; the sides of the interiocking triangles AK, KM, MA and LB, BJ and JL, equal to JM etc. multiplied by $\sqrt{2}$, are the second Aeon and the internal diagonals of the cube JK, AB etc. equal to JM multiplied by $\sqrt{3}$ are the Third Aeon so that the whole creative process, which is expressed in Bond and Lea's Cabala of the Cosmos,[13] takes place within the Mother's womb.1040 is also the gematria of the Greek 'to temenos', the temple precinct, so that this precinct constitutes the microcosm in which the creative process is carried out as a conscious act. Another aspect of this 'mikrokosmos' "is Man, its crown in whom the whole is reflected".

14

CRYSTALS AND MUSIC

We have seen how one of the elements combined together in the Cosmic Scheme is that of crystal structure, with examples drawn from the specific structures of olivine/chrysolite and other silicates and that of aluminium oxides, such as beryl/emerald and ruby. Both Ezekiel, in his reference to "the colour of beryl" and "like the colour of a terrible crystal",[1] and St. John in his reference to a "jasper stone" and "a rainbow around the throne, like an emerald to look upon",[2] make it clear that they understood the significance of crystal structure and the arrangement of particular atoms within the lattice in determining the nature of a given crystal.

We saw the similarity between the Hebrew for 'sapphire', Sammekh Phay Yod Raish, s-ph-r, and 'trumpet', Sheen Phay Raish, sh-ph-r. Phonetically these two words are almost identical and we know that our word 'cipher', a secret language, comes from the Hebrew sh-ph-r, suggesting that the harmonic scale of the trumpet and in particular the Israelite Jubilee trumpet, expresses this secret language. We saw the destructive effect of this sound, the 'Hilel', in the demolition of the walls of Jericho[3] and Jeremiah has an example of its constructive effect, the Hebrew 'Hiel'.[4] These harmonic proportions are expressed in the musical proportions of the Cosmic Scheme.

Figure 39 shows the relationship between the musical proportions, with the base note JK/LM and the iron/magnesium silicate chrysolite, one of the Holy City jewels in Revelation 21. In this illustration four of the silica tetrahedra are shown (1 to 4), with their links to the rectangle JKLM indicated by dotted lines. Figure 40 shows similar links between the musical basis of the Scheme and beryl/emerald and ruby. Like emerald and ruby, sapphire is also a silicate and the phrase "paved work of a sapphire"[5] suggests the crystal lattice within which the atoms of crystals are arranged. The gematria of the Hebrew Lammed

Bayt Nun Tav, 'paved', is 482, while $481 = 37 \times 13$, the gematria of 'e genesis', 'the beginning', hints at the fact that the Scheme is the beginning of the whole physical creation.

Another example of a group of words which, in English, seem unrelated to 'sapphire' and 'trumpet', consists of the verb to write; and the nouns 'book' and 'scribe'; "David wrote a letter"[6] where the word 'wrote' is used to translate the Hebrew Sammekh Phay Raish (s-ph-r) and the same Hebrew word in Deuteronomy 28:61 is translated as 'book', while in 2 Samuel 8:17, the almost identical Hebrew word Sammekh Vav Phay Raish (s-v-ph-r) is translated as 'scribe'. So we have:

Hebrew	English translation
Sammekh Pay Raish	Wrote
Sammekh Pay Raish	Book
Sammekh Vav Pay Raish	Scribe

Put together, these three translations suggest the enscribing of words in a book, the storage of information in an easily accessible form. Coming back to the "paved work of a sapphire", this suggests, as we saw, the crystal lattice, the diamond pattern in the Cosmic Scheme and the picture of the Mother and Child. In modern electronic systems crystals are used in the storage of information and we have already seen indications that the designers of the picture of the Mother and Child understood what we call quantum mechanics. Figure 42 shows the AlephBaytic cube within the Cosmic Scheme and turned through 30 degrees, so that its lattice fits into that of the crystal structure of the whole Scheme. This demonstrates the way in which each letter of the AlephBayt has a place within the crystal structure. By entering particular words, or the roots of words, from the Hebrew text, specific energy patterns can be accessed. This fits with our term 'cipher', 'sifr', which means any Arabic numeral, hence the symbols of the Hebrew AlephBayt, which serve as numbers and letters – this being the basis of gematria and the code derived from it. The Hebrew sh-ph-r, meaning 'trumpet', links the number/letter code with the musical proportions and with the whole Cosmic Scheme.

The Arabic 'sifr' also means 'nothing' and our recent investigation of the atom has revealed that, although it is in a sense composed of sub-atomic particles, it consists largely of what appears to be empty space, that which is implied by the term 'sifr'. In one sense the particles, electrons, protons etc., can be defining this space and some physicists are now more interested in this space than they are in the particles.

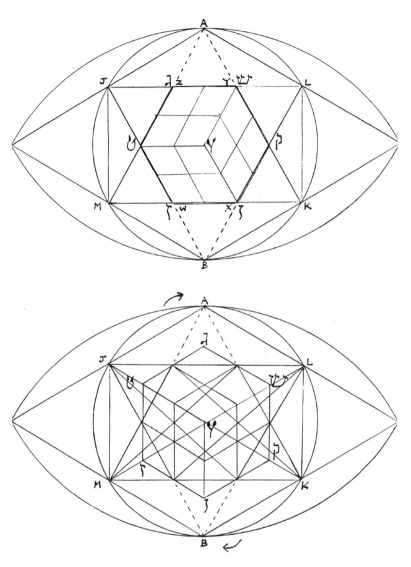

Figure 42.

Bond and Lea, in a discussion of 'To A Mysterion' the First Mystery, refer to Schwartze's translation (into Latin) of the Pistis Sophia. In a discourse on the three robes of Christ, the second Endyma is spoken of as "...the glorious name of mystery...that which is ineffable, which is the great light".[7] We know that the three robes correspond to the three rays and to the three Aeons,[8] which are expressed in arithmetical terms as One and the roots of Two and Three in the AlephBaytic cube. This

121

First Mystery, that of Alpha, is "(also) the last", i.e. it embraces the whole AlephBayt and therefore the whole $2 \times 2 \times 2$ cube and the whole three-dimensional creation. But the Pistis Sophia states that the mystery is 'ineffable', that is 'more than can be expressed'. But that is precisely what is implied by the Arabic term 'sifr', the relatively vast space which contains the sub-microscopic particles that make up the atom.

Here our authors are concerned with "the law which governs the genuine Gematria for the definition of ideas concerning the Nature and Works of God".[9]

"To arrive at this [Law] we have to postulate the powers of the Number Ten being figurative of the Ineffable Source of All, allowing that it may be a fitting symbol of that Ineffable...". This symbolism is developed in the Prima Sephira, where we have:

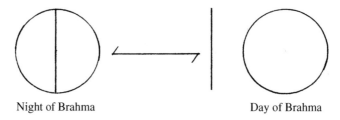

Night of Brahma   Day of Brahma

The term 'Sephira' is essentially a latinised form of the Arabic 'sifr', expressing the nothingness of the resting state, expressed by the Prima Sephira. In Vedic terms, it is the 'night of Brahma'. The 'Day of Brahma' is initiated when the omphalos emerges from the sphere and we have 10, the ten Sephiroth of the Tree of Life, the tenth of these being the physical creation, shown in Figure 34.

Figure 30, from a relief of the young Pharaoh before Amon,[10] shows a different view of the Prima Sephira, in which the single circle of the latter has parted along the line AOB, the omphalos, to form the vesica piscis ABEF, the 'opening of the mouth'. The young Pharaoh and the Tree of Life are contained within the now overlapping circles. They have a diameter of 555 and their circumference is $\pi \times 555$, which is equal to 1746, the gematria of the Greek 'kokkos sinapeos', the mustard seed, "the primal unit of creation",[11] which "grew and became a tree and the birds of the heaven lodged in the branches thereof".[12] Here we have the first stirrings in the 'sifr', with the circle/sphere of nothingness partially separating to form the womb ABEF, and the omphalos AB still contained within it. The creative energy is directed from the right, from Amon's Ankh, entering the system at B. From there it divides, one ray passing through the young Pharaoh's left hand to his throat chakra at E and the other going through his right hand to his third chakra. Left and right suggest Yin and Yang, the bipolar nature of the physical world, which is about to emerge into manifestation and which is symbolised by the $5+5$ sephiroth of the Tree of Life.

This process of manifestation, between the "opening of the mouth' and the descent into the physical, that level of energy which is perceptible to our physical senses, is a hierarchy of descending levels, the rungs of Jacob's ladder. By this means the creative energies reach a slow enough frequency to be apparent to our senses. Physicists try to describe these events in terms of either the 'Big Bang' theory or the 'Steady State' theory. These are regarded as mutually exclusive, but they are not, since the four dimensions of time and space have no meaning in the higher dimensions. So this argument cannot be resolved within the limits of what the disputants call 'reality', that is within the limits of the material world. But once we are prepared to 'step onto Jacob's ladder' and admit that this offers us access to reality, then we discover that we are already at the centre of the solution, standing at 0 in the Cosmic Scheme, in the position of the young Pharaoh in Figure 31, bathed in the life-giving higher energies.

"And I saw a new heaven and a new earth".[13] Here, in the Greek text, 'heaven' appears as 'ouranon', the accusative form of 'ouranos', which Bond and Lea look at on page 10. 'Ouranon' has the gematria of 741 and $740 = 37 \times 20$, which is the gematria of the Greek 'kyklos', or 'cycle', suggesting the circle of the Prima Sephira. 740 is also the gematria of 'ktisis', 'creation', indicating that the passage is describing the creative process. Using the system of numerology applied to the Roman alphabet, where A to I and J to R $= 1$ to 9 and S to Z $= 1$ to 8, then the word NEW has the numerology 555 and this is the diameter of the two overlapping circles in Figure 31 and its repetition confirms that the writer of Revelation is referring to the 'opening of the mouth' in his description of the new creation.

The only other English word consisting of the three letters with the numerology of 5 is 'wen', meaning both 'carbuncle' and 'city' in the sense of "the great wen". Throughout Revelation the symbolic figures which appear outwardly to stand most decidedly in opposition to each other are revealed as being one and the same. The duality which, from the human point of view, obtains universally, is an illusion of this world and exists neither in the world of archetypes nor in their corresponding numbers. The scene of the vision continually shifts, so that at one moment the prophet sees the splendour and corruption of Babylon, followed immediately by the holy city, Jerusalem, with its fresh springs and walls of sparkling crystal . . . Babylon is destroyed, Jerusalem is revealed. But these are not two different cities. According to their numbers they are identical, for the gematria of Babylon and of the holy city Jerusalem is:

$$\text{Babylon} = 1285$$

$$\text{'Ē agya polis ē Jerusalem'} = 1285^{14}$$

And here we have the example in English of these same apparent opposites in the words NEW and WEN, on the one hand the freshness, optimism and idealism implied by the new and on the other, staleness, pessimism and cynicism suggested by the suppurating boil. All this is reflected in the geometry of Figure 31, where the diameter of the overlapping circles is 555. Furthermore, in the Greek text of Revelation 21:1, 'ouranon' (heaven), has the gematria 741 and the Greek 'kyklos' (cycle) is 740: today's Jerusalem is tomorrow's Babylon, an endless cycle of birth, maturation, decay, death and rebirth. However if we choose, we can break the wheel to which we have bound ourselves and spiral upwards to reality: inherent in the number 555, applied to the diameter of a circle, is the multiplication by π to give 1746, the grain of mustard seed like unto the kingdom of heaven. As Bond and Lea say, "The study of the true principles underlying the older symbolism of Numbers is of a very intimate nature and involves a well-founded familiarity with pure mathematical principle in their relation to . . . the cyclic laws governing the motions of the heavenly bodies" and other bodies, ranging from electrons to the orbits of twin stars, in relation to each other and beyond.

Bond and Lea suggest that "a number may state a quality or principle, and at the same time, the defect, or excess, of that quality" and they go on to look at examples of pairs of words in Greek which express these opposite principles.[15] Remarkably, similar examples of pairs of words, only distinguished by the prefix 'a', exist in Sanskrit, for example:

Sanskrit	Greek
Rupa = corporeal	Délos = manifest
Arupa = incorporeal	Adélos = unmanifest

An example of polarity in Hebrew, indicated in the same way, with the prefix Aleph, is:

$$\text{Mem Lammed Aleph Final Khaf} = \text{M-Lak}$$

$$\text{Ayn Mem Lammed Qof} = \text{Am-Lak}$$

Here, although the actual letters differ slightly, phonetically the two words are virtually identical. Malek is translated as 'angel' and Amalek fought against the Israelites (was, in other words, a dark angel).

Another example occurs where although the words are quite different, the polarity is revealed by the gematria:

$$Urim = 550$$

$$Thurim = 549$$

These two components of the breastplate[16] are simply transliterated in the English text and the gematria of 550 and 549 is arrived at by trans-literating them into Greek, suggesting that they impart polarity to the breastplate. Their gematria of 550 and 549 point to the two intersecting circles in Figure 31, whose diameter is 555. The process of 'opening the mouth', in which the circle representing the resting state separates to form the mouth, or womb, the first stage in the active, or creative stage, indicates the polarisation, which is inherent in the physical world. The Urim and Thumim are a part of this process of polarisation. The two fruits held by the young Pharaoh, one in each hand, indicate another aspect of this polarisation, 'left' and 'right'.

In the first verse of the first chapter of Genesis, the central group of the seven groups which make up this verse is Aleph Tav, the first and last letters of the Hebrew AlephBayt before the addition of the five finals. This, as Stan Tenen points out, is not translated in the English text. It is the unmani-fest, resting state represented by the Prima Sephira. In Figure 31 Amon is in the act of writing these letters Aleph and Tav on the on the persée fruits, the two pomegranates. The stylus held by Amon penetrates the outer skin, revealing the red rind underneath. The two letters are shown in the figure.

A key example of polarity indicated by paired words occurs in the English word 'abyss', which is from the Greek 'abyssos'. This occurs in the Greek text of Genesis 1:2, where pneuma (spirit or creative energy) hovers over the abyss, or deep. This word abyss comes from the Greek 'byssos', meaning thread, whose gematria is 1072 and $1073 = 37 \times 29$, 'o theos thē gēs', the god of the earth. So we have:

$$Byssos \text{ 'Thread'} = 1072$$

$$\text{Abyssos 'threadless' or 'without structure' } 1073 = 37 \times 29 \text{ 'the God of the Earth'.}$$

The pneuma, or creative energy hovering over the abyss, or deep, in Genesis 1:2, describes a 'threadless' or structureless state before the descent of the creative energy into three dimensions.

Bond and Lea look at the twenty-first chapter of St. John's Gospel, in which Peter and six disciples go fishing. The free-swimming fish are the energy in a structureless or 'abyssal' state. "That night [the disciples] took nothing" (verse 3). Jesus, standing on the shore tells them to "cast the net on the right side' (verse 6) "...and they were not able to draw for the multitude of fishes". The net is the 'byssos', and Jesus demonstrates the creative art, by which the 'fish' are 'caught', that is the 'Net' imparts a physical structure to the energy, acting as the crystal lattice in which the atoms are 'caught', producing physical substance. "Simon Peter... drew the net to land, full of great fishes, one hundred fifty and three" (verse 11). But why does the text mention this rather odd number? Bond and Lea point out that the gematria of 'to diktyon', the net, is 1224, which is equal to 8×153, while the gematria of 'fishes', 'ichthes', is also 1224. Furthermore, written as one hundred, fifty and three, rather than one hundred and fifty three, points us towards the AlephBaytic cube and the division of the Hebrew letters into the three enneads of single, double and triple figures. Looking again at Figure 2, we see that the letter Nun, whose gematria is 50, is at the centre of the cube, while Ghimel whose gematria is 3 and Qof whose gematria is 100 are at two corners of the cube. Together these three form a hologram, a minimum resolution figure, for the construction of the whole cube. In directing these proceedings, Jesus gives a perfect example of the way in which the Hebrew letters act as creative instruments. Figure 44 shows how the AlephBaytic cube relates to the crystalline basis of the Cosmic Scheme and the way in which the letters can be used to place the appropriate atoms within the lattice, or net, to bring about the manifestation of any given crystal and hence of the whole physical universe.

Bezalel, who built the tabernacle, a cosmic structure, according to Hebrew myth, knew how to use letters as instruments of power. The account of Jesus and the one hundred and fifty and three fishes gives a detailed explanation of how alchemists, himself and Bezalel included, were able and still are able to work with the 'fishes' and the 'net', that is the free, unorganised energies and the organising lattice. Solomon, as one of these alchemists, used his magic carpet, a form of the net, in catching the creative energies in combination with his magic ring, each of whose four jewels was concerned with one of the four fundamental forces (see Figure 23).

One of the remarkable things about Bezalel is his name which, written in Hebrew, has the gematria 153, or "one hundred, fifty and three", embodying, as a hologram, the proportions of the AlephBaytic cube, the very structure that forms the basis of his alchemy (see Figure 2).

"One hundred, fifty and three" is a translation of the Greek 'ekaton pentekonta trion', whose gematria is 2590. This is equal to 37×70 and is the gematria of the Greek 'topos photos', a term occurring in Gnostic texts, translated into English as 'a radiant place', the 'creative source', C in the Cosmic Scheme. It suggests the three robes of light and the source of the seven rays and the Cube of Light. Jesus, standing on the shore of Lake Tiberias in John 21, is directing creative energy from this source in his demonstration of physical manifestation. In his parable of the grain of mustard seed, which "became a tree, so that the birds of the heaven come and lodge in the branches thereof",[17] we know that the mustard seed, 'kokkos sinapeos', has the gematria 1746, the kingdom of heaven and that the tree of life in Figure 31 is contained within two overlapping circles whose circumference is 1746, so that the birds in Matthew 13 are nesting in the tree of life. Like the fishes in John 21, they represent the free, unorganised creative energy and the tree is playing the same role in the creative process as the net in John 21 – so that in 'nesting in the branches', the previously free-flying birds become static, the equivalent of the creative energy caught in the crystal lattice in the process of crystallisation (Figure 43).

The number 1224, which is the gematria of both 'to diktyon', 'the net' and 'ichthes', 'fishes', has other points of interest. As John Michell points out "it is the sum of all the numbers up to 49"[18] and is therefore the number of the magic square of Venus, which consists of the numbers 1–49 arranged in a square block 7×7. We know that the Solomon's magic carpet, ABCD in the Cosmic Scheme, is also, appropriately, the magic square of the Sun and it is the cosmic net in which, for example, the AlephBaytic cube, and its 27 Hebrew letters, each expressing a particular energy, are 'caught'. This gives a hint of the significance of magic squares in general: that each of them expresses a particular harmonic system, each associated with a particular planet and that these are combined to make a vibrational system characteristic of our solar system. As Bond and Lea point out, 153 has a similar property, being the sum of all the numbers 1–17. Astonishingly, the Hebrew for fishes is Dallet Ghimel Yod, whose gematria is 17. In his *Numerology of 1224*, John Michell adds the gematria of 'the net' and 'fishes' making 2448 and, referring to his Figure 31, the 153 fishes in the net, he shows that "2448 is the perimeter of the 'fish' in the net, 16 small rhombuses contained within a larger one, making 17 in all. Given the perimeter of 2448, the width of each small fish is 153".[19]

Bond and Lea discuss the rationalising of irrational forces and give as an example, the Greek words 'sother', 'saviour' and 'ichthys', 'fish'. In

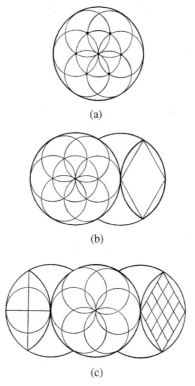

(a)

(b)

(c)

Figure 43. The 153 fishes in the net (John 21). (a) St Peter and six disciples enter a boat. (b) They cast a net on the right side and catch fish. (c) Peter draws the boat and net with fishes to shore.

their diagram on page 52, the diameter of the intersecting circles is 1408 and the sides of the equilateral triangle drawn within them have a length of 1224, the gematria respectively of 'sother' and 'ichthys'. In the Cosmic Scheme these are CF and AB.

We already know that the ratio of the half base to the height, OE:OA is $1:\sqrt{3}$ (see Figure 8) and $1224/2 = 612$, the gematria of Zeus in Greek, while $612 \times \sqrt{3} = 1060$ and the gematria of Apollo is 1061, so that the proportions of Bond and Lea's geometry combine Christian and Greek mythology.

Looking at the musical proportions of Bond and Lea's diagram Figure 8 shows that an equilateral triangle combines the ratio of $1:\sqrt{3}$, AO:CO in Figure 44, with the ratio 8:9, CO:CA, the major wholetone (the notes E:D). Furthermore, we know that CA = JK and LM, the diagonals of the rectangle within which the musical proportions of the Scheme are developed. Therefore, if CA is the base note D, represented

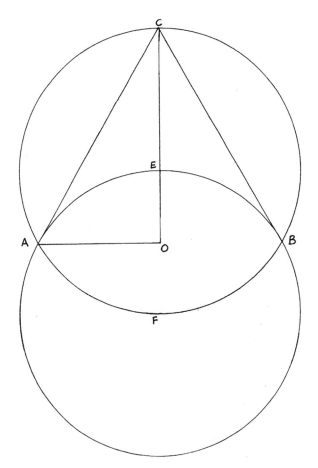

Figure 44. CA corresponds to the base note D, while CO = CA × 8/9, the ratio 9:8, the major wholetone, the note E. This establishes the musical basis of the whole Cosmic Scheme.

by CA in Figure 47, CO, which is shorter, will correspond to a note which is higher and CF, which is longer, will correspond to a note which is lower. We already know that the frequency represented by CO is 8/9ths the frequency of CA, the note E, and CF is 9/8 × CA in length, giving a note which is one major wholetone lower. Therefore Bond and Lea's diagram on page 52 is based musically on three notes with an interval of two major wholetones:

CF	CA	CO
C (33 Hz)	D (37 Hz)	E (41 Hz)

Although they are not concerned with the musical proportions of the geometry, Bond and Lea state that the $2:\sqrt{3}$ ratio expressed by the gematria of 'sother' and 'ichthys' can be expressed geometrically "as the diameter of a circle to the side of an equilateral triangle within that circle" and this geometry clearly demonstrates the ratio of the major wholetone in music. Then, when we put this into the context of the Cosmic Scheme as a whole, the proportions of the wholetones are revealed in the context of the musical proportions of the whole.

We can apply the same ratio of $1:\sqrt{3}$ to the AlephBaytic cube: looking at Figure 1, where each of the sides of the eight cubic modules which make up the cube is equal to 1, then a side of the whole cube is equal to 2 and in the ratio $2:\sqrt{3}$, $\sqrt{3}$ is the internal diagonal of the cube.

Returning to Bond and Lea's discussion of the powers of the Number Ten as "figurative of the Ineffable Source of All", our authors continue: "Ten, in this connection, is the sum of the first four arithmetical powers, $1+2+3+4$, the Tetraktys of the Pythagoreans. These powers first exist as the simple Monad, Diad, Triad and Tetrad".[20] Figure 45 shows what, in Vedic mythology, is known as 'shiva's drum'. This is a double Tetraktys, with the Monad at the centre. Tetraktys, written in Greek, has the gematria 1626 and $1628 = 37 \times 44$, the gematria of the expression "head of the corner", "The stone which the builders rejected the same was made the head of the corner". Here, at the centre of the 'drum', is that 'keystone', without which the whole edifice collapses, the centre D in Figure 48. In Vedic mythology it is the linchpin of Indra's chariot wheel, the birthplace of Agni[21] (see Figure 41), the nearest we can come to the concept of the Creative Source.

Bond and Lea's "four powers" correspond to the tetracord F-C-G-D, either "rising fifths of ratio 2:3, or falling fourths of ratio 3:4", with their reciprocals, D-A-E-B at the opposite end of the drum.[22] The rhythmic patterns played out on the drumskins at each end of the drum interact, reflecting the bipolar nature of our material world, but with the still centre, D, a reminder of the Source. "As on a linchpin, firm, rest things immortal".[23]

Shiva's drum is a pictorial version of Bond and Lea's arithmetic series based on the gematria of 'phonē Kyriou' (the Voice of the Lord), and this voice is that of "one who cries in the wilderness",[24] where the one who cries is, in the Greek, 'o boon',[25] whose gematria is 992, while that of 'tympanon' (drum) is 991, so that Shiva's drum does indeed express the energy emitted from the Creative Source D.

Looking again at the Cosmic Scheme (Figure 10 etc.), we can put Shiva's drum into this context: the equilateral triangles CKL and DJM

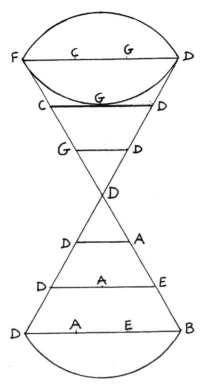

Figure 45. Shiva's drum, with the base note D, the linchpin of Indra's chariot wheel, at the centre, the stone made "head of the corner". The notes F-C-G-D in the upper part of the drum, with their reciprocals D-A-E-B at the lower part. In the Cosmic Scheme, the upper drum-skin lies in the plane KL and the lower one in the plane JM.

each constitute one half of the drum; by hinging them at KL and JM, C and D can be swung, so that they lie at the centre 0. This puts the drum into the musical context of the Scheme, JK and LM having the proportions of the base note of the two octaves underlying the whole Scheme, the note D_1 (37 Hz), the linchpin of Indra's chariot wheel.

Writing of the complex of significant Greek words, whose gematria relate to the proportions of the diagram of the cabala of the fish (p. 54), Bond and Lea write "it is clear however that this amazing cabala refers not only to the Christian Faith and its members, but, by this body of geometrical teaching, to its Founder as well...".[26] But the proportions of the cabala and its associated gematria extend beyond the bounds of any particular belief system and the beings associated with it. Bond and Lea point out that, if the diameters of the intersecting circles in the cabala are equal to 1408, then the long axis of the vesica so formed

(ABEF) is 1219, which they point out is the gematria of 'ichthys' (fishes) But this is also the gematria of 'Sōthis', the Greek name for Sirius. Furthermore, Bond and Lea state that the area of "the greater Rhombus (ABCD in the Cosmic Scheme) [is] 1288, or, by another convention, 1289" and 1288 is the gematria of 'ē theotēs iesou' (the divinity of Jesus). Again, 1289 is also the gematria of Osothis, a form of Osiris. As with so much of the Hebrew text of the Old Testament, we have clear links to ancient Egypt, demonstrating the origins of Judaeo-Christianity in Egypt. As we know, Jesus is in the tradition of the tree god cult exemplified by Osiris and in 2 Samuel 18:9 and 14: "Absolom rode upon his mule, and the mule went under the bows of a great oak/and his head caught hold of the oak, and he was taken up between the heaven and the earth; and the mule that was under him went on.... And (Joab) took three darts in his hand, and thrust them through the heart of Absalom while he was yet alive, in the midst of the oak.... And ten young men...compassed about and smote Absalom, and slew him".[27]

In the above passage, in Absalom rode, the Hebrew for 'rode' is Raysh Khaf Bayt, whose gematria is 222 ($= 37 \times 6$), suggests at once that we are dealing here with cosmic affairs. Then the phrase "between heaven and earth" is a translation of the Hebrew Hay Sheen Mem Yod Sammech Vav Bayt Yod Lammed Hay Aleph Raiysh Final Tsadde, whose gematria is 2774 and $2775 = 37 \times 75$, the gematria of "The word became flesh and dwelt among us",[28] in the Greek text, while "three darts" in verse 14, in the Hebrew text, has the gematria 1556, while $1554 = 37 \times 42$, 'anastasis sarkos', the resurrection of the body. In these two instances we have a remarkable pre-echo of Jesus's crucifixion and resurrection and a clear indication that Absalom caught up in the tree is an earlier version of a similar event. The "ten young men" constitute a reference to the ten sephiroth of the tree of life and "compassed about" the great oak, they suggest that the latter is the tree of life.

15

THE ORIGINS AND CHARACTERISTICS OF GOTHIC ARCHITECTURE

In their Appendix 111, Bond and Lea examine the principles in "the ground plans of churches and other Gothic buildings". In Bond's view the main object "was one of geometrical perfection, the object being the reproduction of the form of the rhombus of two equilateral triangles"...,[1] corresponding to ABCD in the Cosmic Scheme. As we have seen, this principle appears in use much earlier than the first appearance of Gothic, in the early twelfth century, being present in ancient Egypt.

"... from very early times a peculiar respect − even a sanctity − attached to those proportions" based on the double equilateral triangle and its enclosing vesica". "Ye shall do no unrighteousness in judgement, in meteyard, in weight, or in measure".[2] In this passage 'unrighteousness' is the translation of the Hebrew Tav Ayn Sheen Vav, whose gematria is 776 and $777 = 37 \times 21$. This is the gematria of the Greek word 'stauros', meaning 'cross', using the redundant letter digamma. If the cross is drawn, say with its upright equal to 2×7 and its horizontal component equal to 7, this gives the dimensions of a 2×1 rectangle, in which the ratio of the short side to the diagonal is $1 : \sqrt{5}$, or $7 : 19$. This is also the ratio of the central point plus inner ring of 6 to the 19 visible points of the "cube of the Mother", the AlephBaytic cube. This is the ratio of the foot to the megalithic yard (see below).

The next key word in the passage from Leviticus is Bayt Mem Sheen Phay Tayt, translated as 'judgement', whose gematria is 431, while the Greek word 'katabolē', 'conception', has the gematria of $432 = 18 \times 24$, suggesting that the passage is concerned with the creative process. The English translation of the next word, 'meteyard' does not occur anywhere else in the Bible and is not in current English usage. It is a translation of the

Hebrew Mem Dallet Hay, whose root is M-d, derived from the Ancient Egyptian Maet, or Maat, goddess of measure and balance, or equilibrium. It occurs in English in the term 'to mete out', meaning to measure out. This fits with the implication of righteous or fair judgement. The choice by the English translators of the unusual word 'meteyard' is intended to indicate that it is linear measure that is being referred to. The full Hebrew word is Mem Dallet Hay, whose gematria is 49 and the diagonal of a square whose sides are equal to 5 is $\sqrt{49}$, or approximately 7.071, and the diagonal of a square whose sides are equal to 7 is $\sqrt{100}$, or approximately 9.899. "In one of the hymns to the Maruts, 'storm gods', 'healers', and 'Indra's helpers', they are numbered forty nine: "The mighty ones, the seven times seven, have singly given me hundred gifts".[3] As we know, 49 years is the orbital period of Sirius B round Sirius A. This results in a gravitational cycle of 49 years, which is a major factor in our terrestial environment, acknowledged by the Israelite Jubile of 49/50 years (the exact period of the orbit is between 49 and 50 years: we do not have an exact measure, any more than we do for the number of days in an Earth year.

"Of every clean beast thou shalt take to thee seven and seven . . . of fowl also of the air, seven and seven. . . . For yet seven days . . .".[4] Here we have echoes of the passage from the Rg Veda above. The 'animals' and 'fowl' refer to energy patterns being built into the ark, which will form the basis of the post-diluvian world. The Hebrew word translated as 'seven' is Sheen Bayt Ayn Hay, whose gematria is 377 and it occurs five times in this passage, 5×377 being equal to 1885 and $1887 = 37 \times 51$, the gematria of the Greek 'to genos to David', the ancestry of David, extending back to Noah. So the 'seven and seven' suggest the square with sides of seven, McClain's rgvedic cabala for $\sqrt{2}$.

Taking the gematria of the Hebrew word for 'seven', 377, and dividing it as 37 and 7, then 37 and 7 gives the following in gematria: $37 = 1369$, the gematria of the Greek 'o theos goes' (the god of life and 7^2 is 49, $\sqrt{49}$ being the diagonal of the 5×5 square, a value for $\sqrt{2}$. As we saw, $\sqrt{2}$ is an arithmetical solution for the musical discrepancy between the rising and falling notes of an octave and the point at which Agni, the Hindu fire god, is born from the womb of Usas, "daughter of the Sun".[5]

In our day 'measure' is reduced to purely practical needs, so that the use of metric is entirely suitable, but Leviticus 19:35 lifts measurement from the purely practical domain, giving it a cosmic significance. If we look at Figure 1 for example, when the sides of the eight modules which make up the whole $2 \times 2 \times 2$ cube $= 1$, then the diagonals of the faces of these modules, for example, from Zayn (7) to Phay (80), is equal to $1 \times \sqrt{2}$. If the sides of the modules are equal to 1 foot, then:

Table 5.

Unit of measure	Metric equivalent	Ratio	Reference to AB cube
Royal cubit	0.51 metres	$1 : \sqrt{3}$	Zayn Nun
Megalithic yard	0.829 metres	$1 : \sqrt{5}$	Zayn Tav
Yard	0.914 metres	$1 : \sqrt{6}$	Zayn Final Khaf

This demonstrates the holistic nature of proper measure, as opposed to metric, which is simply linear, without any other dimensional implications. The consequences of using metric are plain to see: modern buildings lack any aesthetic quality and good acoustics in auditoriums are achieved by chance, or by a laborious process of trial and error. Through the neglect of the law set out in Leviticus 19:35 we have the breakdown of society in our time.

Having established that the principle underlying the plans of Gothic cathedrals and churches was "one of geometric perfection", Bligh Bond continues "As to the motive which led the ancients to their preference for geometric truth – that is another question"[6] but perhaps we can now attempt to answer that question.

As the relationships between the different units of measure reveal, it is the proportions on which they are based, rather than the exact measurements, that are significant and it is the proportions which underlie the AlephBaytic cube which determine the positions of the atoms in the crystallisation of any given compound and to which the gematria of the text is the key. We know that geometry, crystal structure and musical proportion all combine together in a harmonious whole, which constitutes the whole cosmos. By becoming aware of this and consciously relating to it, we become a part of this whole and achieve harmony in our lives. Figure 40 demonstrates how the proportions of the figures of Mother and Child, with the Mother squatting in a natural position for giving birth and the Child on her knee, fit perfectly with the geometry, musical proportion and specific crystal structures. This combination of geometry, music and crystalline proportion applies to the whole of humanity.

Bligh Bond goes on to discuss "The rhombus or vesica: Not only do we find it reproduced in many approximations in the plans of our own and continental churches, but it is notoriously used in Gothic detail wherever the architectural expression of the best periods reaches its highest point".[7] We know that the occurrence of the rhombus and vesica extends far beyond medieval architecture and that it is universally present, underlying physical form. Figure 25 shows why this is so: in the first stirrings of an active phase within the Prima Sephiroth, the circle separates to form the primary vesica (Figure 25(b)), the 'opening of the mouth'. Then, in Figure 25(c), the Omphalos, the Cosmic Phallus, makes its appearance, the line AB. This corresponds to the radii of the overlapping circles that form the vesica. This appearance of a straight line is a major step in the manifestation of physical form and all straight-line relationships in the natural world relate to it. For example, in Figure 25(f), the sides of the hexagon ALKBMJ, AL, LK etc., are equal to AB/2, as is the note indicated by JM/KL, while the note below, corresponding to MZ, JW etc. is equal to JM × 9/8, the major wholetone ratio in music.

The fundamental part played by the omphalos AB is established in Figure 25(d), where the rhombus is developed within the vesica ABCD, since, the two triangles being equilateral, its sides are equal to AB. These are also equal to the diagonals JK and LM, the base note of the two octaves on which the musical proportions of the Cosmic Scheme are based. All aspects of the Scheme, geometric, musical and crystallographic, are determined by the omphalos.

To find the geometric principle "in its more perfect expression" Bligh Bond looks to "works of the best period.... This would be the 12th century and the early 13th century of English work".[8] It is at the beginning of this period that the Gothic style appears in Europe, fully developed, without any apparent period of evolution, "The Gothic style sprang fully armed from heads that had astonishing knowledge in them".[9] In chapter 6 Charpentier goes into great detail as to how "in the year 1118 nine French knights" arrived in Jerusalem and were given lodgings by Baldwin, the Crusader king of Jerusalem, "in a wing of his palace on the site of the old Temple of Solomon...".[10]

Charpentier bases his account on the work of the Frankish historian Guillaume de Tyre, writing towards the end of the 12th century. Guillaume is by no means entirely reliable,[11] but his account is the basis for all the later versions.[12]

I believe that, as far as his account of the nine knights and their supposed activities on the site of Solomon's temple are concerned, Guillaume's story is a fabrication. Faced with the fact that the style of architecture that we now know as 'Gothic' was in fact already, by the beginning of the 12th century, a fully developed system, employed in the Al Aksar mosque and other Muslim sacred buildings, would have made it completely unacceptable to the Christian Church. So, I suggest, what the nine knights set out to do was to drop hints that they had discovered the secret of the principles on which Solomon had based the design of his temple. This at once transformed what was actually the product of a faith that was challenging the right of the King of Jerusalem, ruler of a Christian kingdom, established after driving out the followers of Mohamed, to reintroduce Christianity to the Holy Land; to an architectural style derived directly from that developed by King Solomon and employed in his temple, the anticedent of the very temple in which Jesus had taught. Thus, rather than archaeologists digging in the remains of Solomon's temple, the nine knights acted as propagandists promoting a new and radical style of architecture.

The impact of the wave of Gothic cathedrals and churches which swept across Europe in the next 150 years was in itself immense, but it was only a part of a movement within the church that was set in motion in order to cleanse Christianity of corruption and venality and free it from complacency. The question arises as to who was behind this movement for renewal within the church. It took place at the same time as a revival of the Cistercian monastic order, under Saint Bernard, who transformed the state of the order from one of near-bankruptcy, to one of immense wealth: by 1153 there were more than three hundred Cistercian abbeys. This extraordinary growth directly parallels that of the Order of the Temple, which was expanding in the same way during the same years.[13]

This parallel development was not by chance: there was a dense web of connections between the two organisations. Behind the growth of both orders "loomed the shadowy presence of uncle and nephew (Andre de Montbard, one of the nine knights and Saint Bernard), as well as the wealth and influence of the Count of Champagne, a member of the Order of the Temple, three of the knights also being vassals of his".[14] There seems to have been "some complex and ambitious overall design ... something was discovered in the Holy Land – something of immense import, which aroused the interest of some of Europe's most influential noblemen... something that had to be kept secret".[15]

Everything points to the fact that this important secret lay in the origin of the Gothic style, in this revolutionary approach to the design and building of churches and cathedrals. One only needs to compare the squat, massive Romanesque with the succeeding Gothic, to be aware of the fundamental change, which led, through the development of plainsong, to a major change in religious observance. The new style was an essential factor in enabling the Cistercians, under Bernard, to attain "spritual ascendancy in Europe".[16] Any hint that the new style might have been lifted wholesale from an Islamic design would have been fatal to the intentions of Bernard and his associates. Its use led to a revival of Christianity.

Charpentier discusses the musical proportions underlying the design of Chartres cathedral[17] and all of these fit with those we have found in the Cosmic Scheme. He shows that the plainsong sung at Chartres and in other Gothic churches uses a musical scale which is specifically designed for the proportions of these buildings. This, together with the soaring vaults and magical effect of the light, has an inspiring effect, which was all part of Bernard's intended revival.

Charpentier[18] has an elevation of the choir at Chartres. He shows the width between the pillars on the north and south sides as "40 half cubits", which he gives as 0.369 metres, and this is the length of 1 remen ($= 14.62$ inches). This distance of 40 remen corresponds to JM in the Cosmic Scheme and the points from which the vault springs corresponds to K and L, the diagonals JK and LM being 80 remen, the octave below. The intervening intervals are not diatonic, but correspond to the special Gothic minor scale.[19]

Charpentier lived in an entirely metric culture, a tremendous disadvantage when dealing with a sacred building, such as Chartres, or indeed for any purpose beyond the merely practical, but, without knowing it, he had stumbled across the remen, his 'half cubit'. In addition, in discussing the width of the choir, "from axis of pillar to axis of pillar, I have chosen the mean of different measurements by different authorities, 16.40 metres, which assumes in practice a measure of 0.82 metres for the builder".[20] But after surveying a large number of henges and barrows, Professor Thom concluded that the unit of measure he had found on all the sites he had surveyed was 0.829 metres, the unit he named the 'megalithic yard'. The French edition of *The Mysteries of Chartres Cathedral* was published in 1966, the year before Thom's *Megalithic Sites in Britain*.[21] Many archaeologists have still not come to terms with the implications of Thom's work for neolithic and Bronze Age archaeology and the presence of the megalithic yard, the remen and other ancient measures in medieval buildings, is virtually unknown. Of course, when the basis of true architecture on the vesica piscis and its contained rhombus is recognised, as Bligh Bond demonstrates[22] and as is clearly shown in Figure 25, then it is apparent that the integrated true measures, with their geometric, crystallographic and musical basis, such as the foot, remen and megalithic yard, are an essential part of architectural design.

Professor Thom also demonstrated the division of a circle into five to give the equivalent of a Gothic arch at the henge at Moel-ty-Uchaf, in

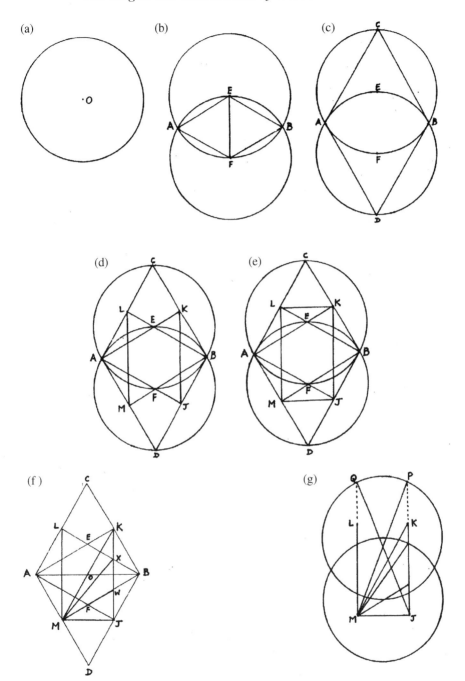

Figure 46. Construction of the Gothic arch from the Cosmic Scheme. MK=the base note. JM is the octave above. JQ and MP=the fourth in the octave below.

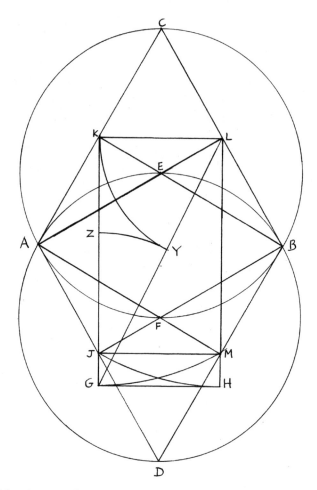

Figure 47. The elevation of the choir at Chartres drawn within the Cosmic Scheme. JKLM represents the elevation of the choir, with the floor at JM. The arcs MG and JH are drawn to give the 2 × 1 rectangle GHKL and the diagonal GL is drawn to give the triangle GKL. An arc with centre L and radius KL is drawn and another with centre G and radius GY. Then the ratio KZ : GZ = 1 : 1.618, the Golden Mean ratio.

north Wales. This can be achieved with nothing more than a peg and line, by extending the geometry to the note F in the octave above, as Charpentier does. Figure 46 shows the development of the Gothic arch from the Cosmic Scheme. Figures 47 and 48 show the method for locating the two lower points of the pentagram, arrived at via the Golden Mean ratio of 1:1.618, which Charpentier does not do. I believe that the former for the vault was laid out on the floor, using Figure 51 as the basis and then lifted into position at K and L.[23]

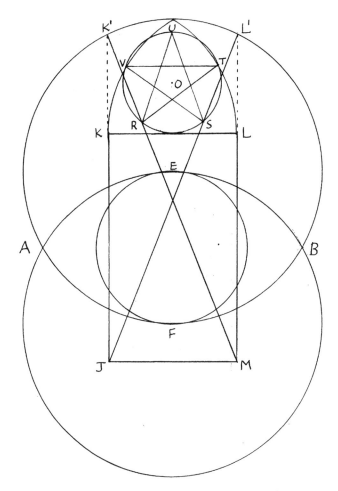

Figure 48. The Pentagram within the Gothic Arch. The circle with centre O and diameter KZ is drawn tangential to KL. JK and ML are extended to K′ and L′, and JL′ and MK′ are drawn to give the lower points of the pentagram. Arcs with centres K and L and radius KL then give the arch, passing through T and V.

"To find the geometrical principle (the double equilateral triangle) in its more perfect expression an examination must be made of the works of the best period. . . . This would be the 12th century and the early 13th century of English work"[24] and it is surely not a coincidence that this is also the period of the building of Gothic cathedrals and churches. "It has been the writer's good fortune to discover an almost perfect example of such a principle in the Lady Chapel of Glastonbury Abbey . . . a plan of this chapel is given from which it will be seen that the figure of the vesica is present in a form so nearly accurate as to leave only the most insignificant margin of error, and the figure is repeated in duplicate on the main axis"[25] (the rest of the building).

In his plan of the Lady Chapel, Bligh Bond shows a vesica piscis drawn to enclose the outer margin of the plan, "But the inner measurement, which is the breadth between the buttress faces on centre of north and south walls, is computed to have been as nearly as possible 37 feet". Therefore, since this is the length of the short axis of this inner vesica (JM in the Cosmic Scheme), the long axis will be $37 \times \sqrt{3} = 64.01$ feet (JL and MK) and the diagonals are equal to $37 \times 2 = 74$ feet (JK and LM). "Allusion may here be made to a remarkable fact noted constantly by the writer in his measurements of the various parts of the fabric of Glastonbury Abbey. . . . It is that the whole scheme of the Abbatial church and buildings appears to be planned upon a series of commensurate squares of 37 feet, or, more accurately speaking, of twice 37, that is, 74 feet.[26]

I have quoted this passage from Bond's *Gate of Remembrance* at length, because, in it, he produces evidence which suggests that the original church on the site of the Mary chapel was founded by Saint Joseph of Arimathaea in 47 CE. If this evidence is correct, then this is, by many years, the earliest known Christian foundation and because the proportions of the Mary chapel are based upon it. This means that the geometric proportions based on the double equilateral triangle which we have seen in 12th to 13th century Gothic cathedrals and churches have origins in Christian architecture more than one thousand years earlier. What we have in the Gothic is master masons working within this 1st century CE tradition and adapting it to the pentagonal design imported by the nine knights from Jerusalem.

The crucial element in the proportions of the Mary chapel based on the measurements 37 and 74 feet is that it hints at the first octave in the series 37:74:148, derived from "time, times and half a time".[27] It is the diagonal of 74 feet which forms the basis of Bond's plan of the whole Abbey. Figure 4 shows one of these squares developed within two vesicae pisces, with their axes at right angles, the four-petalled lotus, the corners of the square, N, P, V and X, are at the points of intersection of the vesicae. This is an outstanding example of a dense interconnection between geometry and gematria, combining feet, inches and megalithic yards. The plan of the Mary chapel also corresponds in its proportions to the rectangle JKLM and the diagonals of this rectangle give the base note of the two octave series JK/LM:JM/KL:JM/2 (the length of the sides of the tetrahedra of silica).

The four-petalled lotus in Figure 4 appears in T. C. Stewart's *The City as an Image of Man as the Founding of an Indian Temple*.[28] "It provides the simplest approximate method of squaring the circle", the area of the circle whose diameter is EF having an area approximately equal to that of the square NPVX. In *The Mystery of the Plan*,[29] Charpentier discusses what he calls the 'three tables', one rectangular, one square and one round, and relates these to significant parts of the plan at Chartres. These all have the same area, which in square megalithic yards is equal to 800. For example, in the case of the rectangular table, on which the plan of the choir is based, "The width of the table is 20 measures of 0.82 metres.... Its length is 40 measures and its surface 800 measures squared, say 537.92 metres squared",[30] 0.82 metres being equal to 1 megalithic yard. Figure 4 shows the round and square tables, the circle with diameter EF and the square NPVX. Charpentier shows how the three tables determine details of the layout at Chartres. For example, he shows how the square and round tables combine not only to locate, but also determine the thickness of the two pillars at the base of the choir and the crossing. Bligh Bond[31] shows how the square table gives the width of the nave and ambulatory at Glastonbury, measured between the insides of the north and south walls and also the positions of the pillars of the nave and choir. The whole plan follows the 74-foot grid. The whole building, except for the Abbot's kitchen, was destroyed in the fire of 1184. Clearly, the rebuilding under Abbot Robert de Jumierges adhered strictly to the same 74-foot grid derived from the Joseph's wattle church of 47 CE.

Charpentier[32] (p. 105) goes on to remark on certain what we would call 'irregularities' in the plan. He cannot explain the reason for these, but considers them to be the expression of "The knowledge that watched over the building". He notes "the irregular placing of the pillars on the south side of the choir and its aisle. The two pillars that frame the bay that contains the sacred centre are further from one another than those of the other bays. While the average of the other bays is about 7 metres, the distance apart of these two is 7.83", the difference of 0.73 being equal to 1 MY [megalithic yard]...this bay opens on the window of Notre-Dame de la Belle-Verrière. Does the explanation lie here? Were they unwilling to restrict in any way the flow of light from this window?" We know from the crystal structure underlying the Belle Verrière (see Figures 40 and 43) that there are strong hints of laser action associated with this stained glass picture. The wider bay opposite this window and between the latter and the sacred centre in the Choir may be designed to allow light energy passing through the window to shine directly on to the sacred centre. Charpentier shows the use of a vertical pole and the shadow of the rising equinoctial sun to orient the original Neolithic long barrow which, in turn, determines the orientation of the cathedral. The sacred centre is at the place where the pole was placed.[33] Critchlow[34] shows in detail this method of orientation, using the method for orientating Hindu temples according to the Manasara Shilpa Shastra. This gives the four-petalled lotus (Figure 4), in which two vesicae pisces at right angles have their long axes oriented north–south and east–west and a square, NPVX, has its corners at the points of intersection between the two vesicae. We found that, at Glastonbury Abbey, this square has an area of 740 MY (megalithic yards). It forms the outer boundary of the sacred enclosure, the 'temenos' in Greek and the gematria of 'o temenos' is 740.

"The elaboration of the plans of Hindu temples from this basic 'squaring' is a ritual expressive of Creation from its source, multiplicity reflecting Unity".[35]

Critchlow continues, "This procedure is a rite in the full meaning of the word, linking the form of the sanctuary as a microcosm to the solar system as a macrocosm". This reveals the full significance of the 1 MY. extra width between the pillars on the south side of the choir: the Sun shining through this gap enacts, at each equinox, the orientation of the neolithic barrow, which determines the orientation of the medieval cathedral built 4000 years later.

Looking again at the light pouring in through the wider bay, on to the sacred centre in the choir, Charpentier states that "The stained glass window and true Gothic are inseparable. Like true Gothic, the [Belle Verrière] window is a product of high science...".[36] It is surely not by chance that the picture of the Mother and Child has been placed in line with the wide bay in the choir and the sacred centre. Figure 40 shows how Bligh Bond's rhombus of two equilateral triangles is developed in relation to the stained glass picture.

In the Belle Verrière we have Bligh Bond's rectangle, formed by the plan of the Mary chapel at Glastonbury, expressed in the underlying geometry of the picture of the Mother and Child, with the rectangle JKLM in Figure 40, with the ratio of its width JM to its length JL being equal to $1 : \sqrt{3}$, corresponding to Bligh Bond's plan of the Mary chapel on p. 100. As Charpentier shows in his elevation of the choir at Chartres,[37] this is also the ratio of the width between the pillars of the nave and the level from which the vault springs. In the plan of the cathedral, the slight tilt of the base of the apse towards the north,[38] allowed the builders to make the width of the bay opposite the sacred centre 1 MY wider than the other bays in the choir and this tilt reflects that of the Mother's head in the picture. The Child's height in the picture, just contained within the length of the rectangle, JM, allowing for the forward rotation of his feet, indicates his part in the design of the building. The diameter of the circle representing the amnion is also equal to JL and, by rotating the Child's feet, the artist has indicated the initial stage of his birth and hence that of the building.

"The superior accuracy of the inner rhombus, based on the interior dimensions of the Mary chapel at Glastonbury", gives us a suggestion of another and closer approximation to truth than the 'Mason's convention' of a ratio of $4:7$.[39] This nearer approach is represented by the ratio $37:64$, or 37 feet:37 royal cubits (1 foot $\times 1.73 = 1$ royal cubit (r.c.)). This "superior accuracy" is necessary since it then gives the diagonals of 74 feet, which form the basis for the grid of 74 foot squares on which the plan of the whole Abbey Church is based. "Allusion may here be made to a remarkable fact noted constantly by the writer in his measurements of the various parts of the fabric of Glastonbury Abbey and that of the other foundations and walls discovered. It is that the whole scheme of the Abbatial church and buildings appears to be planned upon a series of commensurate squares... of 74 feet". As we have seen, this square, NPVX in Figure 4, is combined in the four-petalled lotus; with a circle whose diameter is equal to the length of the short axes of the two vesicae, having the same area as that of the square, Charpentier's square and round tables. We know that this geometry forms the basis for the foundation of Indian temples; putting Bligh Bond's work into a wider context.

Bligh Bond goes on: "The reason for the choice of this number of feet [74] as the unit of general measurement is still [80 years ago] under investigation...". However; the answer was well enough known to organ-builders; who habitually refer to the different pipes by their length in feet; the 2 foot pipe for example; giving middle C (c' in Helmholtz's notation); the four foot pipe giving the note c one octave below; the one foot pipe giving c'' one octave above and so on. We know that these proportions, expressed in feet and inches, are fundamental to the Cosmic Scheme, so that if JM is a pipe 2 feet in length, giving middle C (c'), a pipe of length JW ($= 2$ feet 3 inches), will give a note one major wholetone below, the note b, a pipe of length JK will give the note c and so on. Helmhotz, in the middle of the 19th century, made all this clear but, to the scholastic mind, music was music and measure was measure and any attempt to put them together was abhorrent. For all his profound understanding, Bligh Bond apparently never made the

145

connection, still, to some extent, trapped in the scholastic frame of mind. The lowest common multiple between the foot, the megalithic yard and the yard (= 0.914 metres) is 60 feet, 22 MY/20 yards. This is the distance between the axis of measures and the eastern corner of the Covered Temple at Luxor. This establishes the canon of measures for the whole temple. The overall width of the Covered Temple is 44 MY and the total length of the building is 308 MY, 308/7 being equal to 44, the base note in a harmonic series extending over three octaves. If we take this base note as C (= 66 Hz), then the top note of the three octaves is c'' (528 Hz) and the ratio of MY : musical frequencies in Hertz is 2 MY : 3 Hz (see Figure 33).

16

THE SONG OF THE BOW

Robert Lawlor discusses the Egyptian concept of the 'Neter',[1] which can be translated as 'Founding Principle'. Lawlor states "The principle of the Neter is associated with the cubit. The proof is found in the hieroglyphic system: the sign of the cubit is represented by a section of the forearm assuming the outline of the recumbent sign of the Neter".

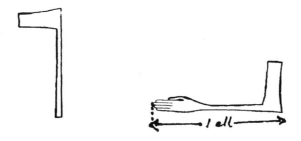

The contrast between these two, the rigid form of the hieroglyph and the complex, flexible human arm reveals the essence of the Neter. The bent position of the arm implies the energy stored in the muscles, expressed when the arm draws the string of the longbow back. Then, when the string is released, all the stored energy of the muscles is expressed in the flight of the arrow.

The distance from the angle of the elbow to the tip of the second finger in an adult is 18 inches, or half an English yard (0.458 metres). Under 'ell' in *Skeat, The Oxford Etymological Dictionary*, he gives "Icelandic, alin, the arm from the elbow to the tip of the middle finger", hence we have the ell.bow, the bent arm giving the measure of an ell, with all its implications of stored energy. This same tension in relation to, for example, the dimensions of the Gothic arch at Chartres, expressed in Charpentier's 'Chartres Cubit' (the double remen of 0.738

metres), illustrates the difference between proper measures, such as the foot and the remen, as compared to the purely practical metric system.

Bligh Bond suggests the use of what he calls an ell at Glastonbury, a unit of 37 inches, which suggests a double ell ($= 2 \times 18\frac{1}{2}$ inches), but it is so near a yard ($= 36$ inches) that this seems unlikely. In any case Bond does not put forward any evidence in support of his suggestion.

"And [David] bade them teach the children of Judah the use of the bow: behold, it is written in the book of Jasher".[2] This is one of the most extraordinary passages in the whole Old Testament, firstly because of the reference to the book of Jasher, one of only two in the whole Testament. For some reason this book was excluded from the Hebrew text. Secondly, although most of the revisions made to the 1611 text in 1885 are very minor, here the two texts are radically different: while the 1611 text gives 'use of the bow,' translating the Hebrew Hay Nun Hay as 'use', the revisers in 1885 give 'song'. Both versions seem correct, 'use' suggesting the practical aspect of the longbow as a weapon and 'song' perhaps hinting at the drawn string as producing a note when plucked. In the former, the drawn string emphasises the energetic implications of the ell.bow, with the arm drawing the string being bent to its maximum and the arm holding the bow being fully extended, prior to the explosive release of the arrow, releasing all the locked-up energy of the bent arm. The extent to which the bowman is able to draw back the string, and therefore the degree to which he can bend the bow, determine the force exerted on the arrow and this is indicated by the length of arrow between the string and the back of the bow, a reference to the matter of measure and the ell.

The unusual aspects of this passage from 2 Samuel 1 do not end here: the word 'bow' in Hebrew is Qof Sheen Tav, whose gematria is 800, that of the Greek word 'choinix' (measure), confirming the link with the bow and the ell.bow. Then, the insertion of the passage, completely out of context, at the beginning of David's lamentation for Saul and Jonathan, acknowledged in the 1611 version by brackets, in itself very unusual, suggests a direct quotation from Jasher, inserted at random. All this points to the fundamental link between proper units of measure (as opposed to the purely practical metric) and creative or destructive energy expressed by the Hebrew Hiel and Hielel. The presence of the constructive Hiel in sacred buildings, such as Chartres cathedral, is inherent in their proportions and is evoked by, for example, plainsong chant, which evokes creative resonances, bathing the congregation and lifting their conscientiousness to higher planes.

"Another adjustment... offering a near approach to the rhombic ratio (of $1 : \sqrt{3}$) is that of $11 : 19 ...$".[3] In his chapter VIII, Lawlor discusses

"The Egyptian Canon for a Standing Man".[4] One method "divides the height of the entire man into 19 units". Schwaller shows this applied to a relief showing the young Pharaoh, from Room 20 of the Temple of Luxor. A grid of 19×19 is applied to the figure, with the top of the grid cutting the top of the Pharaoh's head and the top of his Uraeus. The eleventh square coincides with the position of the navel, which thus divides the body by 1 and $\sqrt{3}$. Bligh Bond is referring to the $11:19$ proportion in churches and cathedrals, while Schwaller shows its occurrence in the human figure, but we have seen how the latter combines the two (see Figure 29). Here, with the figure of Pharaoh superimposed on the plan of the temple, the position of the navel marks the centre of the inner court, marked also by his belt at the back. "According to the measurements recorded at Luxor, and based on a great number of other monuments", the division into 19 units, gives 3 units for the length of the foot[5] (Lawlor, p. 116). The distance from the axis of measures, marked in the stones under the pavement of the Covered Temple at Luxor, to its eastern corner, is 60 feet, giving a distance in 3/19ths of the Pharaoh's height of 60/3, or 20, suggesting that these units also apply to the plan of the temple. But 3 feet equal 1 English yard, so that Schwaller's units of 3/19 are in fact yards (1 yard = 0.916 metres). 831 is the gematria of the Greek word 'pyramis', the overall length of the temple being 832. The Hebrew for 'rod', in this case in the sense of measuring rod, is Mem Tayt, whose gematria is 49 and $17 \times 49 = 833$, confirming the idea of the rod as a means of converting between different units of measure, in this case feet, megalithic yards and English yards ($20:22:60$ between the axis of measures and the eastern corner of the Covered Temple). If the rod is the omphalos contained within the circle in the Prima Sephira of the tree of life, then we have a circle whose diameter is 49 and $\pi \times 49$ ($22/7 \times 49) = 154$ and "One hundred, fifty and three"[6] gives the gematria of the Hebrew letters Qof, Nun and Ghimel, the letters at the centre and two of the corners of the Aleph-Baytic cube, a holograph from which the whole cube may be constructed. Bezalel, the builder of the Hebrew tabernacle,[7] whose name in Hebrew is Bayt Tsadde Lammed Aleph Lammed also has the gematria of 153, suggested that the Israelite master masons followed the Egyptian tradition. In Israelite mythology Bezalel "knew how to use letters as instruments of power", that is he was able to use the energies embodied in the letters to give form to sacred buildings, which would have cosmic proportions and would promote harmony among the people using the buildings. All this fits with the concept of measures, such as the ell, being themselves expressions of creative energy.

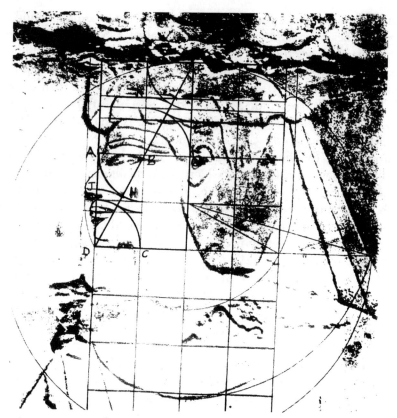

Figure 49. Golden Mean proportion and the human head. Within the eight-square grid on the front of the head, the diagonal OF is drawn. Then, AD, BC, EB and FG are divided by the Golden Mean, so that, for example, the ratio AJ:OJ=1:1.618, locating the head band at K and L, the tip of the nose at J and the lips at M.

Figure 49 shows an enlargement of the head of the Pharaoh from the relief in Room 20 at Luxor.[8] The rectangles ABCD and EFGB show how such 2×1 rectangles may be divided by the Golden Section ratio of 1:1.615; in ABCD, for example, the diagonal BD is drawn, the arc with centre B and radius AB is drawn to cut the diagonal at H; the arc with centre D and radius DH is drawn to cut AD at J and the ratio AJ:JD is 1:1.618. This reveals that all the major features of the head are based on the Golden Ratio. This ratio occurs throughout the Aleph-Baytic cube, in the rectangle Hhayt (8), Final Phay (800), Final Nun (700) and Zayn (7); Final Phay (800), Raish (200), Qof (100) and Final Nun (700). This illustrates the way in which Bezalel and other masters could manipulate the energies contained in the letters to produce the appropriate proportions in the resulting three-dimensional form. These are expressed in the spatial arrangement of the atoms in the resulting crystals.

As a complementary ratio to that of 11:19, Bligh Bond discusses one of 19:33. "Take 33 inches as your 'yard' ".[9] But 40 years later Alexander Thom arrived at a measure of 0.829 metres as the principal unit employed by the builders of neolithic and Bronze Age monuments and 0.829 metres is 32.63 inches. Clearly Bond had deduced the existence of what Professor Thom called a megalithic yard and Charpentier called "a measure" 40 years before either of them. This remarkable insight has lain unregarded ever since.

Bond states "We are dealing with a proportion which...bears to the 12-inch foot the approximate relation of $\sqrt{3}:1$".[10] He refers to this measure as a cubit; it is in fact Schwaller's royal cubit of 20.64 inches (= 0.524 metres). In the Cosmic Scheme, if JM = 1 foot, then JL = 1 r.c. the proportions would appear as below expressed in units of three inches.

Foot	Cubit	Yard
4	7	12

But we can fill in the gaps now.

Foot	Remen	Cubit	Megalithic yard	Yard
4	5	7	11	12

John Michell[11] has a continuous series, based geometrically on a 1 remen square. Charpentier[12] has the following:

	Feet	Cubits	Megalithic yard
Width of the choir	49	20	18
Length of the choir	115	50	45
Length of the nave	225	100	90
Length of the transepts	202.5	90	81
Height of the vault	115	50	45

These measures are not exact, since they are based on the roots of numbers ($\sqrt{2}$, $\sqrt{3}$ etc.). Exact measure is not the primary concern, but rather the harmony expressed in the proportions of the building and it is this which gives the cathedral and gothic churches in general, their inspiring quality, something that Bligh Bond is aware of, without being quite sure why.

Charpentier asks, "What is this cubit of 0.738 metres? Quite simply, it is the hundred thousandth part of the [circumference of the Earth at the] latitude of Chartres". Peter Tomkins[13] shows a similar relationship between the proportions of the Great Pyramid and the Earth. Charpentier[14] shows a similar relationship between the measure used by the builders of Reims and Amiens cathedrals and their latitudes. This fits with Bond and Lea's exposition of the relationship between macrocosm and microcosm based on the gematria of the relevant terms in Greek.[15] A harmonious resonance between building and planet is essential to the proper working of a sacred building and the Earth, the other planets and the stars. Sir Norman Lockyer[16] gives examples of the relationship between temples and stars. Bligh Bond's grid on which he bases the plan of Glastonbury, consists of squares of 74 feet and their area is 740 MY,[17] while the gematria of the Greek 'aitheros melos', the music of the spheres, is 740 $(= 37 \times 20)$, a strong hint of a similar link with the macrocosm at Glastonbury.

Bond states that "the principal measure employed by the builders of antiquity" is "the cubit of 7 palms"[18] the 'palm' presumably being the 'hand' of 4 inches, used to measure the height of a horse at the shoulder. However, Alexander Thom concluded that the megalithic yard of 0.829 metres was the principle measure used in neolithic and Bronze Age structures, such as henges. The truth is that all these ancient structures, including medieval buildings, such as Chartres, are based on the vesica piscis and the rhombus which it contains." The ratio of width to length of the vesica is $1:\sqrt{3}$, so that, by their nature they must involve the use of at least two measures of equal importance. At Glastonbury, for example, Bond gives the inner rhombus, contained within St. Mary's chapel, a width of 37 feet, giving the ratio (of breadth to length) of $37:64$ (feet),[19] or 37 feet to 37 royal cubits. Charpentier's rectangular table at Chartres measures 16.40×32.80 metres, or 55×110 feet.[20] Its diagonal is 55 MY, the ratio of foot to megalithic yard being $1:\sqrt{5}$. All the dimensions of such buildings, henges, long barrows, churches etc., consist of an interweaving of all the proper measures, whose interrelationships are based on the roots of numbers. These, of course, reflect the same relationships present in the AlephBaytic cube, which imparts these ratios to the creative energies expressed in the three-dimensional structure.

In the practice of architecture which is based on these integrated measures, such as the foot, remen, royal cubit and megalithic yard, rather than the modern method, which is based on metric measures and is concerned entirely with practicalities, the building is a perfect microcosm, working harmoniously with the whole creation. An example of the way it works is in the relationship between plan and elevation. For example, at Chartres, the choir is contained within the rectangle JKLM in the geometry of the Belle Verrière window and in the Cosmic Scheme, JM giving the width of the floor and JL determining the height of the spring of the vault. The proportions of the latter are determined by the proportions of the musical fourth in the next octave.[21]

"...the foot [royal cubit] and yard...happen to be in the strictest sense of the word geometrical measures – that is to say, measures of the earth's axis". Charpentier (p. 119) shows that his 'Chartres cubit' (a double remen of 29 inches, or 0.738 metres) is Earth-commensurate, being "the hundred thousandth part of the degree of the parallel (of latitude) of Chartres".[22]

Charpentier's 'cubit', the double remen of 29 inches and its use at Chartres, is an expression of a very ancient tradition: the Egyptian Pharaoh Akhenaten transferred his capital from Thebes to the new city of Akhet-Aten. In doing so "Akhenaten intended to cut at the root of the power of the priests of the Temple of Amon in Thebes, who through their control of the national oracle, identified with the god of this temple, had usurped the royal functions.... The new city which was intended to replace Thebes as the capital and geodetic centre of Egypt.... The new capital...was set at latitude $27° 25'$ north, at the middle point between the nothern most point Behdet and the southern limit of Egypt at $24° 00'$".[23] Previously the centre had been at an omphalos in the Temple of Amon at Thebes, "in the main room" where the meridian $25° 42'$ east, the official eastern boundary of Egypt, crosses latitude $26° 42'$ north. Akhenaten reverted to the predynastic geodetic system, based on the geographic cubit of 25.62 inches. Whereas Thebes was 2/7ths of the distance from the Equator to the Pole; the new capital was at the geodetic centre of Egypt.

All this shows that, in the past, the profound importance of placing sacred buildings at geodetically significant points was well understood. Undoubtedly the builders of the neolithic long barrow, which determined the placing, units of measure used and the orientation of Chartres cathedral understood, like their contemporaries in Egypt, the profound importance of geodetics for the proper functioning of the building.

"The prime object of the use of mean proportionals [essentially shapes] in measures would appear to be to provide a standard of area of square form, from which other spaces of equivalent area might readily be derived".[24] The square with sides of 74 feet derives from the diagonal of the Mary Chapel and which forms the basis for the plan of the rest of the Abbey, is an example of this. Figure 4 shows how two of these "mean proportionals", the square of 74 feet and a circle of approximately the same area are derived from two vesicae pisces with their axes at right angles. "I think we must see in the 'squaring of the circle', the search for a 'gate' a key to the passage from one world to another; a secret of initiation in some sense".[25] "Enter ye in by the narrow gate: for wide is the gate, and broad is the way, that leadeth to destruction and many be they that enter in thereby. For narrow is the gate, and straightened the way, that leadeth unto life, and few be they that find it".[26] The Greek word for 'gate' is 'pyle' and its gematria is 518, which is equal 37×14. This is also the gematria of the Greek 'oi kletoi', the Elect, hence those few who find the gate. Furthermore, the phrase "Israel, mine elect", written in Hebrew, is Vav Yod Sheen Raish Aleph Lammed Bayt Hhayt Yod Raish Yod, and its gematria is 777 ($= 37 \times 21$), the gematria of 'stauros', the Cross, that narrowest gate of all.

"The screen, which closed the choir, was two fathoms and nine inches wide, approximately 4.20 metres, it is therefore likely that it filled the space between the pillars at the base of the rectangular table".[27] Apart from the unusual manner of stating the distance, in fathoms and inches, which would usually be given as 12 feet nine inches, this distance, expressed in inches is 153, the number of fishes in the net in John 21 and these may be regarded as a version of the Elect. The rood screen acted as a barrier between the general public and the priests, only the latter being allowed through the screen into the choir, so that essentially, the screen may be equated with the fishing net in John 21. In the Hebrew temple, only the high priest could enter the most holy place, or Debir, and only then after very careful preparations: "And he that is high priest and that is consecrated to put on the garments";[28] "The priests...shall enter into my sanctuary. And it shall be in to the gates of the inner court, they shall be clothed with linen garments...and they shall have linen breeches upon their loins.... And when they go forth into the outer court...they shall put off their garments wherein they minister".[29] "And it came to pass, when the priests were come out of the holy place, that the cloud filled the house of the Lord, so that the priests could not stand to minister by reason of the cloud...".[30] The term 'cloud' is used to describe an energy field, what we might describe as an electron cloud, the radiation from a radioactive source. In the Hebrew text, 'cloud' is Vav Hay Ayn Nun Final Nun, whose gematria is 831, the same as the Greek 'pyramis', where 'pyr' suggests fire, or high energy, a characteristic of temples. The exclusion of the congregation from the inner part of churches suggests the persistence of this tradition long after the energy source had faded.

In the Great Pyramid the circle and square are combined in three-dimensional terms: "The appearance of the π ratio is . . . clearly manifest in the design because the ratio of the base perimeter [8 times the half base, or 55 units of 4 royal cubits (= 2.1 metres)] to the vertical height is 2π, which means that that [the length of the perimeter] is equal to the circumference of a circle whose radius is the vertical height of the Pyramid.

17

THE VEDIC AND EGYPTIAN ROOTS OF CHRISTIAN ARCHITECTURE

As we have just seen, "there is evidence of the highest antiquity for the practice of obtaining equal areas with diverse proportionals. It is found in the ancient Indian 'Shilpa Shastras' or rules of religious art".[1]

In fact the Manasara Shilpa Shastra is profoundly concerned with the whole process of establishing links with the flow of creative energy into the body of the Earth and her creatures: the oracle centres, temples, churches and other sacred buildings. "Our speculations as to how stone circles were laid out in a pre-documented period are based on evidence of the earliest written temple orientation procedures. These, to the best of our knowledge are found in an ancient Hindu manuscript, the Manasara Shilpa Shastra".[2] Keith Critchlow goes on to describe the procedure in detail, arriving at "the 'squaring' of the circle of heaven" (p. 31), which corresponds to the four-petalled lotus, shown in my Figure 4, relating to Bligh Bond's plan of Glastonbury Abbey. This, together with Charpentier's application of the same method at Chartres, persisted in Medieval Europe. Critchlow goes on to show that the same procedures were employed in the laying out of stone circles in Britain in the neolithic and bronze ages, dating from approximately the same time as the Manasara Shilpa Shastra. This "practice of obtaining equal areas with diverse proportionals",[3] underlies the design of all these sacred spaces and thus they act, as Charpentier says as gates, "keys to the passage from one world to another", passages which, like Jacob's ladder,[4] allow the creative energies (= angels) to flow up and down between the different dimensions.

Professor Alexander Thom shows the marvellously elegant geometry underlying the neolithic and Bronze Age henges, all, as Keith Critchlow shows, laid out in accordance with the method established in the Manasara

Shilpa Shastra.[5] The rough stone megaliths making up these monuments confirmed the archaeologists in their belief that the builders were primitive savages. One of Thom's great achievements was to demonstrate that they were, in fact, artists of great wisdom, capable of work that is quite beyond our materialistic society.

The roots of numbers "would appear to have been among the more guarded traditions of the ancient builders".[6] In fact the concept of 'roots' may not have been developed. In the development of the underlying geometry of the henges, each step follows on from the last and may be carried out with a peg and line, so that the underlying mathematical theory need not be ennunciated. Such a method enables the master mason to become a conscious part of his work, unlike the modern architect, who allows the rational blueprint to stand between the design and its execution.

"In the case of medieval workers; however; there does not at present appear sufficient evidence that their object was the equalising of the areas of floor or wall space". In the 80 or so years since Bligh Bond wrote this, evidence has been discovered which suggests the medieval workers regarded the equalising of space as a major part of their objective. Charpentier[7] demonstrates the presence of rectangular, square and round 'tables' of equal area as a major factor in determining the plan of Chartres cathedral. Furthermore, the area of these tables is 800 square megalithic yards. 800, 800 and 800 suggesting the gematria of Jesus, written in Greek, 888 ($= 37 \times 24$), the three visible sides of Bond and Lea's Metacube. Looking again at the Belle Verrière window (Figure 40), we saw that the picture reveals the moment of the birth of the Child, with the breaking of the waters in the Mother's womb. This moment, symbolising the physical manifestation of Jesus indicated by the three visible sides of the Metacube, is expressed in the presence of the three tables in the plan 8(00), 8(00) and 8(00).

Remarkably, it is by applying the method of the Shilpa Shastra, in combination with the foot and the megalithic yard, to Bligh Bond's own work at Glastonbury, that we find an example of the "equalising of floor space" on the plan of the Abbey Church (Figure 4). The application of the Shilpa Shastra method in a medieval building not only demonstrates the 'squaring of the circle', but puts medieval Christian architecture into this very ancient Indian tradition.

"The triangular ratio does not appear definitely in Egyptian monuments".[8] In fact Schwaller de Lubicz's Pharaoh and Queen on the plan of the temple at Luxor (Figure 31) does show the triangular ratio. The overall length of the temple in feet is 832.5 feet and this is exactly contained within two overlapping circles whose radius is 277.5 feet ($3 \times 277.5 = 832.5$). These same overlapping circles underlie the relief of the young Pharaoh before Amon (Figure 30). Here, the two circles with a diameter of 555 feet and centres at E and F, give the rhombus ABCD, in which the ratio AB:CD is equal to $1:\sqrt{3}$. The distance AB, and therefore the length of the sides of the two equilateral triangles, is 481 feet, which equals $555/2 \times \sqrt{3}$ and 481 is the gematria of the Greek 'ē genesis', the beginning. We have this suggestion of the temple as the source of creative energy underlying the physical world.

"Egyptian monuments... follow the laws of the numbers 2 and 5 and their roots – the proportions... of the right-angled triangle (two of) whose sides are as 2:1 and the hypotenuse consequently $\sqrt{5}$...". We find this in the rectangular table at Chartres, whose dimensions of 20×40 MY and orientation, determine these in the medieval cathedral built 3000 years later. Figure 51 shows the same 1×2 rectangles and their $\sqrt{5}$ diagonal in relation to the features of the Pharaoh's face. Docxy[9] shows the same underlying proportions in the human face and body in general.

Bond refers to "the proportions of the first Hebrew temple with its single and double square areas, the Holy of Holies and the Most Holy Place"[10] and Bond and Lea refer to the former. "The Jewish Holy of Holies, the Debir (DBIR)", whose gematria is 216, or $6 \times 6 \times 6$, giving the dimensions of the elevation as well as the plan.[11] The altar in Hebrew is Mem Zayn Bayt, whose gematria is 49, or 7×7. If we assume that the latter is measured in remens (1 remen $= 1.2165$ feet, or Charpentier's measure of 0.369 metres) then, within the double square of 6×12, using megalithic yards (1 remen $\times \sqrt{5} = 1$ MY) the ratio of the dimensions of the altar to those of the containing Debir is $1:\sqrt{5}$.

Figure 50 shows an enlargement of the plan of the inner part of the temple at Luxor, with the superimposed head and trunk of the pharaoh. This shows the double square of the Covered Temple RSTU, with its outer end marked by the outer side of the inner (south western), wall of the Court of Amenhotep the Third. We know that C marks the point at which the axis of measures cuts the inner wall of the Covered Temple[12] and the distance CS is:

10 fathoms = 20 yards = 22 megalithic yards = 60 feet

so that this distance is the datum on which the dimensions of the whole plan our based.

Then the width of the Covered Temple, RS $= 2 \times$ CS $= 44$ MY and its length $= 2 \times 44 = 88$ MY. Taking the triangle RTU and drawing an

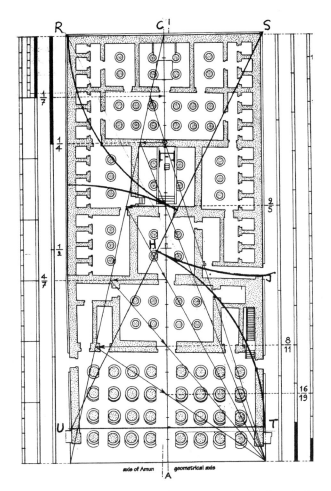

Figure 50. The covered Temple at Luxor. The geometry for dividing the long sides of the double square of the plan, RSTU, by the Golden Mean ratio. In the triangle STU the arc with centre U and the radius TU is drawn to cut SU at H; then the arc with centre S and radius SH is drawn to cut ST at J. The ratio JT:JS=1:1.618, the Golden Mean ratio. This is repeated with the triangle SRU. The construction picks out various significant points on the plan.

arc with centre T and radius TU to cut RT at H, then a second arc, with centre R and radius RH, cuts RU at J and the ratio JU to JR is 1:1.618, the Golden Ratio. 88/1.618 = 54.37 MY, the distance RJ and 88 − 54.37 = 33.63 MY, which is JU. This is very nearly a Fibonacci series of 34:55:89 and would be exact if the Covered Temple was 89 MY long. (Each number in this series is the sum of the previous two

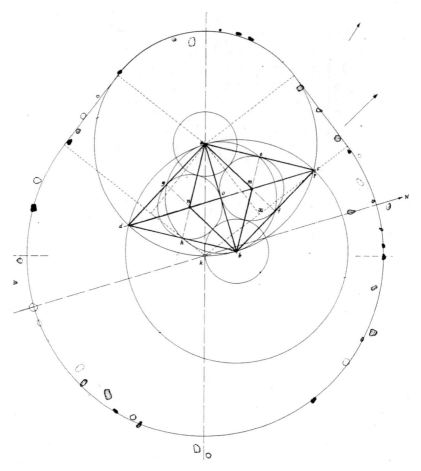

Figure 51. The Cosmic Scheme geometry applied to the henge at Borrowstone Rig. The rhombuses abcd and abmn correspond to ABCD and ABEF in the Cosmic Scheme. These then link with the crystallographic basis in which, for example, in the ruby crystal, a, b, m and n are the sites of aluminium atoms. This atomic structure, established in the geometry, sets up a resonance with the stones around the perimeter. These energies are then radiated into the surrounding countryside.

numbers, $34 + 55 = 89$, and the ratio of each successive pair of numbers expresses the Golden Ratio, so that $34:55$ and $55:89 = 1:1.618$).

Charpentier quotes Jomard and Flinders Petrie as giving a length of just over 230 metres for the length of the side of the base of the Great Pyramid[13] and W. R. Fix (1978) also gives just over 230 (230.36525 metres). In fact it measures 440 r.c. and the square table at Chartres has sides of 44 r.c., exactly 1/10th the size of the Great Pyramid. Each of the two squares which make up the double square of the plan of the Covered Temple at Luxor have sides of 44 MY, giving a ratio between the squares at Chartres and at Luxor of 7:11 (see the scale of proportions, p. 183). Regarding the figure of the Pharaoh, Schwaller de Lubicz divides the figure into 19, his canon humaine. "The crown of the skull which counts as 1, is then removed [at the height of the bandeau of the crown, see Figure 50]; there remain 18 for the height...". Dividing 18 into 7 and 11, the ratio of royal cubits to megalithic yards, locates the navel. This is shown in Figure 51, with the line passing through the Pharaoh's belt at the back.

Bond states that "Some measures are strictly geometric.... Others are in mathematical relation with these".[14] But this distinction between geometrical and mathematical seems artificial and unhelpful: they all relate to each other as the roots of numbers, as exemplified by the $2 \times 2 \times 2$ AlephBaytic cube, where unity is represented by the length of the sides of the eight cubic modules which make up the whole cube and all the proportions, diagonals of the faces, internal diagonals of the modules etc. equal the length of the side multiplied by $\sqrt{2}$, $\sqrt{3}$ etc. Stan Tenen's discovery of the cube of Hebrew letters adds immensely to the significance of Bond and Lea's work.

Bligh Bond continues, "Many [of these measures] are ascertained to have a counterpart in the measures of the human frame". We have seen that the ell relates to the distance from elbow (ell.bow) to the tip of the longest finger, 18 inches, or half a yard. The fathom is the distance from finger-tip to finger-tip when the arms are extended sideways "the two systems, co-exist, blend and harmonise. But we must make our choice as to those which we deem original, and those which we think derived". This assumes an evolutionary process, which would still be the conventional view applied to a study of this kind. However, if we look at the role of Bezalel, who, according to extra-Biblical Hebrew mythology, used letters as instruments of power, then we have a system, based on the AlephBaytic cube, which appears fully developed, without any apparent proceeding evolutionary process. This is all part of the wisdom and understanding handed down from higher dimensions and contained in texts such as the Bible. Gematria provides the key to that understanding.

Furthermore, I do not believe that we are dealing with two systems, between which we have to choose. Bligh Bond suggests a measure of 33 inches (0.837 metres), but does not suggest that such a measure was actually used. In fact Professor Thom demonstrated the existence of just such a measure (the megalithic yard of 0.829 metres) in neolithic and bronze age sites all over the British Isles and the rest of north-west Europe and Charpentier found a measure of 0.83 metres at Chartres. In the AlephBaytic cube, if the length of the sides of the eight cubic modules, which make up the whole cube, have a length equal to 1 remen (1 remen = 0.369 metres), then the diagonal of the faces of each module will be 1 royal cubit, the diagonal of the faces of a double module will equal 1 MY and so on, so that there is no question of the primacy of one measure, nor of one system, since they all form an integrated whole.

Figure 51 shows Keith Critchlow's geometric analysis of Professor Thom's plan of the henge at Borrowstone Rig, in Midlothian, Scotland. Critchlow explores "the possibility for 'founding' the geometry under-lying this henge which would be similar in principle to the ancient Vedic method recorded in the Manasara Shilpa Shastra.[15] This means that the diameter of the primary circle of the Vedic method (centre o, diameter ab) is the same as the radius of the smaller circle as suggested by Professor Thom in the establishing of this circle (centre b, radius ab)". Thom gives $15\frac{1}{2}$ MY for ab, which is equal to 42 feet (42.42 feet exactly). The fact that the measurement in feet only differs from Thom's in megalithic yards by less than 5 inches in 42 feet and that it comes out in whole numbers, while Thom resorts to half and quarter megalithic yards, suggests that the builders used feet as their primary unit. This is confirmed by the dimensions of the rhombus abcd: the ratio ab:cd is $1:\sqrt{3}$ and $\sqrt{3} \times 42 = 72$ feet, while the ratio nm:ab $= 1:\sqrt{3}$, and $42/\sqrt{3} = 24$ feet. This is the distance nm and the diameter of the four small circles with centres at a, m, b and n. Of these four, the one with centre b cuts the vesica abcd at k and the line ak establishes the long axis of the whole henge, at an angle of 17 degrees west of north, orienting the henge to the star Deneb. Professor Thom shows the same orientation to Deneb at the henge at Moel-ty-Uchaf near Bala, in north Wales.[16] In northern Majorca, in the Balearic Islands, a henge was oriented to the Southern Cross constellation. In about 1700 BCE, the Southern Cross ceased to be visible from this site and the henge was abandoned. This suggests the significance of the stellar orientation of these monuments.

Figure 51 shows that the heart of the geometry consists of the two $\sqrt{3}$ rhombuses abed and abmn, with ab as the axis common to both. In the Cosmic Scheme these correspond to ABCD and ABEF, which in turn, links to the crystallographic basis, in which, for example, in Figure 40, in ruby crystals and other forms of corrundum, a and b, m and n, are the sites of aluminium atoms. This atomic pattern in the geometry is, in turn, linked to the atomic patterns in the crystals that make up the stones set out round the perimeter of the henge. It is not by chance that the positions of so many of the stones are determined by alignments within the geometry; with the crystalline composition of the blue and green stones that caused the builders of Stonehenge to bring them all the way from south Wales to Salisbury Plain. It is the pattern in which the atoms are arranged in the crystals which make up the stones, together with the arrangement of the stones in the henge, that underlies its function in organising and distributing the energies entering from higher dimensions, maintaining health and harmony in the surrounding countryside.

Alexander Thom's meticulous surveys of the henge sites, together with his analysis of the Euclidian geometry, provide new insights into the purpose of these magnificent monuments. By putting Thom's work into the Vedic context of the Manasara Shilpa Shastra, Keith Critchlow has put the henges into a global context and revealed the immense skill demonstrated by the builders. Lyie Borst, one-time professor of physics at the University of New York,[17] showed that, like Chartres, Canterbury Cathedral and other cathedrals and churches are based on the plans of neolithic and bronze age henges. Borst shows that in all the examples he investigated, these underlying henge plans conform to one of Thom's four types of layout based on the circle, "the ellipse, two types of 'flattened' circle and egg-shapes developed from right-angled triangles".[18] Borrowstone Rig (Figure 51) is an example of the last of these. One of the cathedrals looked at by Borst is Wells, where the henge was another of Thom's egg-shapes. Borst shows that the plan is based on two circles, of 5 and 7 MY diameter respectively. All the principal dimensions of the present medieval building are based on these two measures. The plan of the Lady Chapel, at the eastern end of the present building, still follows the outline of the underlying henge.

Looking at henge monuments, such as Stonehenge, Avebury, or Borrowstone Rig, it is easy to follow the conventional view promoted by most archaeologists, that these structures composed of rough stone megaliths are the work of primitive and ignorant people. This reinforces our view of ourselves as the product of a process of continuous and increasing enlightenment. However, Alexander Thom's work and Keith Critchlow's revelation of the underlying geometry, show that these ancient structures are the work of people with the highest level of understanding and skill.

18

CONCLUSION

The science of gematria, as I have shown it here, presents a completely different view of the process by which the physical universe is manifested from that proposed by conventional science. The latter refuses to consider the possibility that phenomena outside the range of our physical senses may exist and insists that the three-dimensional world is the product of entirely random processes. 'Science', as it is generally understood, is the product of learning more and more about less and less, so that for example, a succession of particle accelerators, each exponentially more expensive than its predecessor, is leading the study of particle physics up a blind alley.

The study of gematria introduces a completely different view of creation, in which that which is manifest to the physical senses is the expression of a hierarchy of energies, which extend towards infinity with ever-increasing frequencies. As anyone who has got this far with this book will realise that, far from constituting a discreet area of study, gematria is a holistic science, impinging on every aspect of our world and our understanding of it.

As devout Christians and Greek scholars, Bligh Bond and Simcox Lea naturally chose the Greek text of the New Testament and the Gnostic books, such as the Pistis Sophia, associated with early Christianity, as the source material for their investigation, although they make it clear, by several references to Hebrew, that they were aware that Hebrew letters, like those of the Greek alphabet, serve as numbers, as well as phonetic symbols, so that gematria also underlies the text of the Hebrew sacred texts.

Bond and Lea also make it clear that they were aware that several letters from the earlier Greek alphabet had become redundant when "The Greek alphabet was perfected at Athens about 400 BC". What they could not have known was the significance of the loss of the three

164

redundant letters which they show on page 6, reducing what had been three enneads of nine letters each to three ogdoads of eight each.

It was only with Stan Tenen's proposed AlephBaytic cube that the possible significance of this loss to the Greek version became apparent some sixty years after the publication of the first edition of *Gematria*. However, although Tenen was aware that his $2 \times 2 \times 2$ cube contained 27 points, one for each letter of the AlephBayt, he was concerned with establishing a base 3 code, associated with the three axes of symmetry of the cube, rather than with any link with gematria. Looking back to Figure 1, it is clear that, while Tenen's base 3 code works with the axes, the three groups of nine letters works equally well with three parallel planes within the cube and this at once introduces a new dimension to Bond and Lea's work. They refer to "certain entities", such as the relation of the Square root of Two to Unity, or the area of the Equilateral Triangle to that of the square on the same base (see my Figure 13, p. 31), which are aeonial, in the sense of being deeply rooted in the construction of things seen. The AlephBaytic cube, with its complex of relationships between Unity expressed as the length of the sides of the cube to the roots of One, expressed in the diagonals of the faces of the cube and its internal diagonal etc. perfectly expresses these "aeonial entities". This reveals the link between the gematric code and (1) crystalline structure (2) musical proportion and (3) geometry, so that the Hebrew text is revealed as an alchemical source book, giving an insight into the whole creative process. This is not to say that Bond and Lea were unaware of the significance of the cube. They give a brilliant exposition of the cube of light, based on the gematria of the "seven churches which are in Asia" and "the seven stars" in the Greek text of Revelation 1:4 and 16, in which the lengths of the rays which make up the hologram of the cube of light, where Unity $= 100$, add up to 697/8, the gematria of these two phrases.

Furthermore, the second of the three cubes making up the Meta-cube, the Cube of Two, is the Cube of the Mother, the $2 \times 2 \times 2$ Aleph-Baytic cube, but there is no indication that Bond and Lea were aware that this cube has 27 points, one for each letter in the AlephBayt. One can only speculate as to what impact this would have had on their work if they had made this discovery, instead of Stan Tenen, forty years later.

REFERENCES

Introduction

1. Stan Tenen, *The Meru Foundation*. Unpublished material
2. Anne Macauley in Bond and Lea, *Gematria*
3. Revelation 22:13
4. Bond and Lea ibid. Page xi
5. Exodus 3:14
6. Bond and Lea ibid. Page xi
7. Exodus 35:30–32
8. John 21:11
9. Hebrews 8:2
10. Bond and Lea ibid. Pages 8–9
11. Bond and Lea ibid. Page 112
12. 1 Kings 6:20
13. Bond and Lea ibid. *The Method of Gematria*. Page 1
14. Bond and Lea ibid. Page 10
15. Matthew 13:32, Mark 4:32 and Luke 13:19
16. Bond and Lea ibid. Page 10

Chapter 1

1. Bond and Lea, *Gematria*. Page 12
2. Bond and Lea ibid. Page 14
3. Bond and Lea ibid. Page 14
4. Bond and Lea ibid. Page 54
5. Genesis 28:12
6. Bond and Lea ibid. Pages 15–17
7. Carlos Suare, *The Cypher of Genesis* (Stuart & Watkins)
8. Bond and Lea ibid. Page 20
9. Bond and Lea ibid. Pages 30–34
10. Bond and Lea ibid. Page 74
11. Revelation 4:4, 5:8 and 14, 11:16 and 19:4
12. Peter Plichta, *God's Secret Formula* (Element). Pages 113–123
13. Bond and Lea ibid. Pages 21–23

14. Robert Temple, *The Sirius Mystery* (Sidgwick & Jackson)
15. Bond and Lea ibid, page 23

Chapter 2

1. Bond and Lea, *Gematria*. Page 27
2. Revelation 1:4 and 20
3. Bond and Lea ibid. Page 54
4. Exodus 28:33
5. Ezekiel 1:10
6. Numbers 2:3, 10, 18 and 25
7. Stirling *The Canon* (Garnstone). Figure 5, page 37
8. Genesis 49:9
9. Hosea 10:11
10. Genesis 49:9
11. H. P. Blavatsky, *The Secret Doctrine* Vol. 1. Page 379
12. Bligh Bond, *The Gate of Remembrance* (Blackwell) Figure 13
13. *Encyclopedia Britannica*, Volume 20. Page 877
14. Charpentier, *The Mysteries of Chartres Cathedral* (RILKO/Thorsons). Page 101
15. Stirling ibid. Page 34
16. Revelation 21:16 and 17
17. Ezekiel 1:5
18. Exodus 26:1
19. Bond and Lea ibid. Page 75
20. Revelation 21:17
21. Bond and Lea ibid. Page 74
22. Genesis 22:17
23. Schwaller de Lubicz, *The Temple of Man* (Inner Traditions Press)
24. 1 Kings 7:13 and 14
25. Bond and Lea ibid. Pages 29–30
26. Exodus 35:35
27. John 21:6

Chapter 3

1. Bond and Lea, *Gematria*. Page 30
2. Genesis 4:1 and 2
3. Suares, *The Cypher of Genesis*. Page 22
4. Daniel 7:25
5. Bond and Lea ibid. Pages 27–30
6. McClain, *The Myth of Invariance* (Shambala). Page 85
7. Bond and Lea ibid. Page31
8. Exodus 18:1
9. Blavatsky, *The Secret Doctrine* Vol. 2, page 465
10. Matthew 3:16
11. Revelation 8:10 and 11
12. John 2:18 and 21
13. Bond and Lea ibid. Pages 32–33

14. Genesis 22:17
15. Suares ibid. Page 21
16. Genesis 3:22
17. Genesis 22:15 and 17
18. Genesis 6:4
19. Bond and Lea ibid. Page 60
20. 2 Samuel 18:9 and 14
21. 2 Samuel 12:24
22. Bond and Lea ibid. Pages 34 and 35
23. Blavatsky ibid. Page 541
24. Bond and Lea ibid. Page35
25. Bond and Lea ibid. Page 36
26. Temple, *The Sirius Mystery*. Pages 130–131
27. Genesis 3:1
28. Epistle to the Ephesians 1:22
29. Genesis 28:12
30. Genesis 28:18 and 19
31. Temple ibid. Plate 12, page 139
32. Michell, *The View Over Atlantis* (Garnstone Press) Page 94
33. Temple ibid. Page 130
34. Bond and Lea ibid. Page 36
35. Temple ibid. Page 130
36. Psalms 110:4
37. Baigent, Leigh & Lincoln, *The Holy Blood and the Holy Grail* (Cape). Page 187
38. Bond and Lea ibid. Page 38
39. Temple ibid. Page 168
40. Bond and Lea ibid. Page 35

Chapter 4

1. Bond and Lea *Gematria*. Page 42
2. Plichta, *God's Secret Formula* (Element Books). Pages 116–117
3. Bond and Lea ibid. Page 38
4. Bond and Lea ibid. Page 42
5. Doczy, *The Power of Limits* (Autumn Press)

Chapter 5

1. Bond and Lea, *Gematria*. Pages 42–43
2. Graves, *The White Goddess* (Faber). Page 233
3. Bond and Lea ibid, page 42
4. Revelation 8:10
5. Bond and Lea ibid, page 43
6. Bond and Lea ibid, page 43
7. Tenen, *The Meru Foundation*, unpublished material
8. Plichta. *God's Secret Formula*. Page 119
9. Bond and Lea ibid. Page 44
10. Revelation 1:12–14

11. 2 Samuel 18:14
12. Bond and Lea ibid. Page 27
13. Bond and Lea ibid. Page 43
14. Revelation 1:8 and 13
15. Exodus 25:31–33
16. Bond and Lea ibid. Pages 53–60
17. Bond and Lea ibid. Page 33
18. Revelation 1:8 and 22:13
19. Revelation 1:13
20. Bond and Lea ibid. Page 27
21. Bond and Lea ibid. Page 12
22. Isaiah 11:1
23. Job 15:8
24. Numbers 11:24–26
25. Bond and Lea ibid. Page 43
26. Bond and Lea ibid. Page 74
27. Bond and Lea ibid. Pages 45–46

Chapter 6

1. Bond and Lea, *Gematria*. Pages 43–50
2. Bond and Lea ibid. Page 27
3. Bond and Lea ibid. Page 43
4. Job 15:6
5. 1 Samuel 7:16
6. Temple, *The Sirius Mystery*. Page 144
7. Martin Bernal, *Black Athena* (Free Association Books)
8. Bond and Lea ibid. Page 35

Chapter 7

1. Bond and Lea, *Gematria*. Page 47
2. 1 Samuel 28:6
3. 1 Samuel 16:14
4. Exodus 28:15
5. Daniel 12:7 etc
6. Bond and Lea ibid. Page 35
7. Exodus 28:21
8. Bond and Lea ibid. Page 67
9. Daniel 12:7
10. 1 Kings 6:20
11. Bond and Lea ibid. Pages 53–59
12. Bond and Lea ibid. Page 58
13. John 2:19
14. Bond and Lea ibid. Page 4
15. Bond and Lea ibid. Page 5
16. Bond and Lea ibid. Page 42
17. Revelation 1:13

18. Bond and Lea ibid. Page 25

Chapter 8

1. 1 Kings 6:12 and 13
2. Bond and Lea, *Gematria*. Pages 42–43
3. 1 Kings 4:29
4. Bond and Lea ibid. Page 66
5. 1 Samuel 6:14
6. Stirling, *The Canon*. Figure 22, page 271
7. Ezekiel 1:13
8. Ezekiel 1:20
9. Ecclesiastes 1:6, quoted by Blavatsky, *The Secret Doctrine*, Vol. 2, page 553
10. Bond and Lea ibid. Page 66
11. Revelation 1:13
12. John Michell, *The City of Revelation* (Garnstone Press)
13. Numbers 9:16
14. Ezekiel 1:13 and 14
15. Michell ibid. Page 93
16. Bond and Lea ibid. Page 48
17. Bond and Lea ibid. Page 54

Chapter 9

1. Bond and Lea, *Gematria*. Pages 54–58
2. John Michell, *The View Over Atlantis*. Page 25
3. Michell ibid. Page 117
4. Michell ibid. Pages 92–94
5. Bond and Lea ibid. Page 79
6. Michell ibid. Pages 115–116
7. Exodus 28:4 and 5
8. Schwaller de Lubicz, *Le Temple de l'Homme*, Vol. 3, plate XXVI, page 100
9. Graves, *The White Goddess*. Pages 102, 201, plate xxvi, page 100
10. Schwaller de Lubicz ibid. Op. cit
11. Robert & Deborah Lawlor, *The Temple of Man* (Autumn Press)
12. 2 Samuel 8:13
13. 2 Samuel 12:24
14. Bond and Lea ibid. Page 54
15. Bond and Lea ibid. Page 58
16. Temple, *The Sirius Mystery*. Pages 206–208
17. Temple ibid, quoting E A Wallis Budge, *Osiris and the Egyptian Resurrection*, Vol. 2, page 311
18. 2 Samuel 8:13
19. 2 Samuel 12:24
20. Bond and Lea ibid. Page 42
21. Bond and Lea ibid. Page 76
22. 2 Samuel 12:25
23. Temple, *The Sirius Mystery*. Page 185
24. Bond and Lea ibid. Page 58

25. Plichta, *God's Secret Formula*. Page 167 etc
26. Plichta ibid. Table 1, page 33
27. Bond and Lea ibid. Page 60
28. Bligh Bond, *The Gate of Remembrance*. Figure 15
29. Michell, *The City of Revelation*. Figure 28, page 88

Chapter 10

1. Ezekiel 1:10
2. Bond and Lea, *Gematria*. Page 42
3. Ezekiel 10:14
4. 1 Kings 8:7, 10 and 11
5. 1 Kings 1:40
6. 1 Kings 16:34
7. Joshua 6:2
8. Joshua 6:3–5
9. 1 Samuel 4:5
10. 1 Samuel 4:3
11. 1 Samuel 4:19 and 20
12. 1 Samuel 5:3 and 4
13. 1 Samuel 6:16
14. 1 Samuel 6:4
15. 1 Samuel 17:40 and 49
16. 1 Samuel 17:49
17. Temple, *The Sirius Mystery*. Plate 19, page 168
18. Temple ibid. Page 175
19. 1 Samuel 17:43
20. Temple ibid. Page 144
21. Temple ibid. Plate 12
22. Genesis 8:7
23. Exodus 7:9 and 10
24. Charpentier, *The Mysteries of Chartres Cathedral*
25. Temple ibid. Figure 23, page 146
26. Charpentier ibid. Page 92
27. Charpentier ibid. Page 102
28. Exodus 32:15
29. Bond and Lea ibid. Pages 30–32

Chapter 11

1. Bond and Lea, *Gematria*. Page 42
2. Bond and Lea ibid. Page 49
3. Stirling, *The Canon*. Page 120
4. Genesis 1:1
5. Stirling ibid. Page 117
6. Revelation 1:8
7. Stirling ibid. Page 119
8. Exodus 35:35

9. Bond and Lea ibid. Page 32–33
10. Stirling ibid. Page 119
11. Plichta, *God's Secret Formula*. Pages 40–41
12. Revelation 1:8
13. Plichta ibid. Page 136
14. Plichta ibid. Page 132
15. Revelation 1:13

Chapter 12

1. Revelation 4:1–7
2. Ezekiel 1:10 and 13
3. Ezekiel 1:28
4. Bond and Lea, *Gematria*. Page 10
5. Ezekiel 1:22 and 26
6. Revelation 21:20
7. 1 Kings 6:7
8. Bond and Lea ibid. Page 32
9. John 2:19 and 21
10. Ezekiel 1:16
11. Ezekiel 1:22
12. The Song of Solomon 7:1
13. The Song of Solomon 7:2
14. Bond and Lea ibid. Pages 27 and 29
15. Bond and Lea ibid. Pages 29 and 30
16. Bond and Lea ibid. Page 54
17. Bond and Lea ibid. Page 76

Chapter 13

1. McClain, *The Myth of Invariance* (Shambala). Page 81
2. McClain ibid. Page 83
3. Revelation 4:6 and 7
4. Ezekiel 1:13–17
5. Leviticus 13:48
6. Revelation 4:6
7. Daniel 12:7
8. Revelation 4:2 and 3
9. Bond and Lea, *Gematria*. Page 85
10. Blavatsky, *The Secret Doctrine*, Vol. 1, page 210
11. Blavatsky ibid. Page 392
12. Bond and Lea ibid. Page 85
13. Bond and Lea ibid. Page 85

Chapter 14

1. Ezekiel 1:16 and 22
2. Revelation 4:3

3. Joshua 6:4
4. Jeremiah 4:5
5. Exodus 24:10
6. 2 Samuel 11:14
7. Bond and Lea, *Gematria*. Page 47
8. Bond and Lea ibid. Pages 25–28
9. Bond and Lea ibid. Page 49
10. Schwaller de Lubicz, *Le Temple de l'Homme*, Vol. 3, figure xxvi
11. Michell, *The City of Revelation*. Page 85
12. Luke 13:19
13. Revelation 21:1
14. Michell, ibid. Page 144
15. Bond and Lea ibid. Pages 92–93
16. Exodus 28:30
17. Matthew 13:31 and 32
18. Michell ibid. Page 96
19. Michell ibid. Pages 96–99
20. Bond and Lea ibid. Page 49
21. McClain, *The Myth of Invariance*. Pages 84–85
22. McClain ibid. Page 45
23. *The Rg Veda* 1.35.6. Quoted by McClain ibid page 47
24. Isaiah 40:3 and Matthew 3:3 etc
25. Bond and Lea ibid. Page 37
26. Bond and Lea ibid. Page 54
27. 2 Samuel 18:9 and 14
28. John 1:4

Chapter 15

1. Bond and Lea, *Gematria*. Page 98
2. Leviticus 19:35
3. *Rg Veda* 5.53.17 Quoted in McClain, *The Myth of Invariance*. Pages 98–99
4. Genesis 7: 2–4
5. McClain ibid. Pages 83–84
6. Bond and Lea ibid. Page 98
7. Bond and Lea ibid. Page 99
8. Bond and Lea ibid. Pages 100–101
9. Charpentier, *The Mysteries of Chartres Cathedral*. Page 44
10. Charpentier ibid. Page 47
11. Runciman, *A History of the Crusades*, Vol. 2, page 447
12. Lincoln *et al.*, *The Holy Blood and the Holy Grail*. Pages 36–37
13. Lincoln *et al.*, ibid. Page 61
14. Lincoln ibid. Page 59
15. Lincoln *et al.* Page 62
16. Lincoln *et al.* Page 62
17. Charpentier ibid. Page 128
18. Charpentier ibid. Page 134
19. Charpentier ibid. Page 135

20. Charpentier ibid. Pages 88–89
21. Alexander Thom, *Megalithic Sites in Britain*
22. Bond and Lea ibid. Pages 99–101
23. *RILKO Newsletter* no. 19. Autumn 1981. Pages 9–14
24. Bond and Lea ibid. Pages 101–103
25. Bond and Lea ibid. Pages 100–102
26. Bligh Bond, *The Gate of Remembrance*. Figure 13
27. Daniel 12:7
28. Michell, *The City of Revelation*. Page 88
29. Charpentier ibid. Pages 91–93
30. Charpentier ibid. Page 93
31. Bligh Bond ibid. Figure 13
32. Charpentier ibid. Page 105
33. Charpentier ibid. Page 92
34. Critchlow, *Time Stands Still*. Pages 23–31
35. Critchlow ibid. Page 30
36. Charpentier ibid. Page 138
37. Charpentier ibid. Page 134
38. Charpentier ibid. Page 104
39. Bond and Lea ibid. page 102

Chapter 16

1. Robert & Deborah Lawlor, *The Temple in Man*. Page 61
2. 2 Samuel 1:8
3. Bond and Lea, *Gematria*. Page 104
4. Lawlor ibid. Pages 115–127
5. Lawlor ibid. Page 116
6. John 21
7. Exodus 36:1etc
8. Lawlor ibid. Figure 47 page 120
9. Bond and Lea ibid. Page 104
10. Bond and Lea ibid. Page 105
11. Michell, *The City of Revelation*. Page 106
12. Charpentier, *The Mysteries of Chartres Cathedral*. Page 119
13. Tomkins, *Secrets of the Great Pyramid*
14. Charpentier ibid. Page 92
15. Bond and Lea ibid. Page 85
16. Norman Lockyer, *The Dawn of Astronomy*
17. Bligh Bond, *The Gate of Remembrance*. Figure 13, page 148
18. Bond and Lea ibid. Page 105
19. Bond and Lea ibid. Page 102
20. Charpentier ibid. Page 92
21. Charpentier ibid. Pages 134–136
22. Charpentier ibid. Page 119
23. Tomkins ibid. Page 336
24. Bond and Lea ibid. Page 106
25. Charpentier ibid. Page 101

26. Matthew 7:13 and 14
27. Charpentier ibid. Pages 104–105
28. Leviticus 21:10
29. Ezekiel 44:15–19
30. 1 Kings 8:10 and 11

Chapter 17

1. Bond and Lea, *Gematria* Page 106
 2. Critchlow, *Time Stands Still.* Page 29
 3. Bond and Lea ibid. Page 106
 4. Genesis 28:12
 5. Thom, *Megalithic Sites in Britain* and *Megalithic Lunar Observatories*
 6. Bond and Lea ibid. Page 106
 7. Charpentier ibid. Pages 91–111
 8. Bond and Lea ibid. Page 107
 9. Doczy, *The Power of Limits*
10. Bond and Lea ibid. Page 107
11. Bond and Lea ibid. Page 9
12. Lawlor, *The Temple in Man.* Pages 80–82
13. Charpentier ibid. Page 94
14. Bond and Lea ibid. Page 108
15. Critchlow ibid. Figure 28, Page 45
16. Norman Lockyer, *Stonehenge and other British Stone Monuments Astronomically Considered*
17. Lyle Borst, *Nature*
18. Critchlow ibid. Pages 32–33

BIBLIOGRAPHY

Baigent, Leigh and Lincoln, The Holy Blood and the Holy Grail, Cape, 1982

Bernal, M., Black Athena, Free Association Books, 1987

Blavatsky, H.P., The Secret Doctrine, Theosophical University Press, 1970

Bligh Bond, F., The Gate of Remembrance, Blackwell, 1917

Bligh Bond, F., and Lea, F.S., Gematria, RILKO/Thorsons, 1977

Critcholow, K., Time Stands Still, Gordon Fraser, 1979

Doczy, The Power of Limits, Autumn Press, 1979

Graves, R., The White Goddess, Faber, 1961

McClain, E., The Myth of the Invariance, Shambhala, 1978

Michell, J., The View Over Atlantis, Garnstone Press, 1969

Michell, J., The City of Revelation, Garnstone Press, 1972

Plichta, P., God's Secret Formula, Element Books, 1997

Schwaller de Lubicz, R. A., Le Temple de l'Homme, Imprimerie Schindler, Cairo, 1949

Schwaller de Lubicz, R. A., The Temple of Man, Inner Traditions Press, 1998

Schwaller de Lubicz, R. A., The Temple in Man, translated by Robert and Deborah Lawlor, Autumn Press, 1977

Stiling, W., The Canon, Garnstone, 1974

Suares, C, The Cipher of Genesis, Stuart and Watkins, 1970

Temple, R., The Sirius Mystery, Sidgwick and Jackson, 1976

Thom, A., Megalithic Sites in Britain, Oxford, 1967

Thom, A., Megalithic Lunar Observatories, Oxford, 1971

INDEX

179